NARNIA

C. S. LEWIS
AND HIS WORLD

David Barratt

D0472513

7B-14-07-C4

T1-BLW-959

© 2005 Lion Hudson plc/Tim Dowley & Peter
Wyart trading as Three's Company

Published in the United States by Kregel
Publications, a division of Kregel, Inc.,
P.O. Box 2607, Grand Rapids, Michigan 49501.

ISBN 0-8254-2017-2

All rights reserved. No part of this publication
may be reproduced, stored in a retrieval
system, or transmitted in any form or by any
means—for example, electronic, photocopy,
recording—without the prior written
permission of the publisher. The only
exception is brief quotations in printed
reviews.

1 2 3 4 5 6 09 08 07 06 05

Design copyright © 2005 Lion Hudson plc/
Tim Dowley & Peter Wyart trading as
Three's Company

Designed by Peter Wyart

Worldwide co-edition organized and
produced by
Lion Hudson plc
Mayfield House
256 Banbury Road
Oxford OX2 7DH
England
Tel: +44 (0) 1865 302750
Fax +44 (0) 1865 302757
email: coed@lionhudson.com
www.lionhudson.com

Printed in Singapore

Picture acknowledgments

BBC: pp. 5, 7, 8 bottom, 10–11, 13, 17, 19, 21
Douglas Gilbert: pp. 6, 8 top, 33, 44, 47, 51
Alan Parry: pp. 1, 3, 9, 15, 23, 25
By permission of The Marion E. Wade
Center, Wheaton College, IL: pp. 29, 30, 31,
34, 55, 63, 67, 71
Peter Wyart: pp. 35, 36, 39, 45, 48, 49, 59, 60,
65, 66, 68, 76

Contents

The Narnia Stories

L EWIS ONCE REMARKED HE did not enjoy the company of small children. Elsewhere he explained this in terms of shyness. Nor did he have any children of his own; he was not even an uncle, though he was a godfather. He and his brother took in for a short while some children evacuated from London in World War II. By the time he did "inherit" stepchildren, Lewis had already written the Narnia stories. Writing academic and theological books, even science fiction, with no children around him seems an unlikely preparation for a writer whose stories still vie with those of Tolkien, Enid Blyton, and J. K. Rowling for top sales. We might remember another Oxford don who was single—Lewis Carroll—but even he had in mind a particular child to whom to tell the Alice stories. We must look elsewhere for explanations.

In fact, we must look back to Lewis's own childhood reading, and to moments of "joy and desire" that came through such reading. In a sense it was for "the child within" that Lewis wrote, creating the sort of stories he himself would have liked as a child. As an adult, Lewis much preferred to read or re-read good children's books than light adult fiction, especially children's books by such writers as E. Nesbit and Beatrix Potter and Kenneth Graham's *The Wind in the Willows*.

A Mixed Reception

The actual writing of the seven *Narnia* stories happened over a short space of time, between 1949 and 1953. Lewis read the first, *The Lion, the Witch and the Wardrobe*, to a group of friends at Oxford called the Inklings. He had a rather mixed reception, his friend J. R. R. Tolkien not liking it at all. This seems surprising at first, since Tolkien's book *The Hobbit* would appear to have obvious affinities. But *The Hobbit* had grown out of years of Tolkien's constructing an imaginary world, for which he had created myths, legends, histories, and a geography, as well as several languages. There was none of this for Lewis: Narnia suddenly appeared. Tolkien felt Lewis was somehow cheating, and this was not the way a secondary world of fantasy ought to be constructed. Also, Tolkien took a scholar's interest in his world; Lewis did not—it came from the depths of his imagination, often emerging from it in the form of vivid and haunting images.

There is a debate about the order in which the Narnia books ought to be read. The early Penguin editions stated the "correct" order as *The Lion, the Witch and the Wardrobe*, followed by *Prince Caspian, The Voyage of the Dawn Treader, The Silver Chair, The Horse and his Boy* and finally *The Magician's Nephew* and *The Last Battle*. This represents the original order of writing, and of publication by Geoffrey Bles and The Bodley Head, who brought them out more or less one a year from 1950 to 1956. However, Lewis's editor Walter Hooper, in his book *Past Watchful Dragons*, argues we should read them in the order of Narnian time, and that this is how Lewis himself wanted them read. Thus we would start with *The Magician's Nephew*, then work through *The Lion, the Witch and the Wardrobe, The Horse and his Boy, Prince Caspian, The Voyage of the Dawn Treader, The*

A wintry scene from the B.B.C. TV adaptation of *The Lion, the Witch and the Wardrobe.*

Silver Chair and finish with the ending of Narnia in *The Last Battle*. At first sight this seems a completely different order, but really it is only the order of *The Magician's Nephew* we need argue about. The current editions of the *Chronicles* adopt this order. There is a fuller discussion of this question in several of the websites devoted to C. S. Lewis.

It is also interesting to note how the illustrator of the *Chronicles*, Pauline Baynes, quite a young and inexperienced artist to start with, developed her own style through the series. Lewis maintained a good working relationship with her throughout. The American paperback editions (published by Macmillan) lack many of her illustrations, and their absence is very apparent.

Lewis's Imagery

Whatever the merits of Hooper's argument, we shall discuss the books in their order of first publication. We have mentioned that various images often shaped the story which followed. One such image was of "a Faun carrying an umbrella and parcels in a snowy wood." Lewis first had this image when he was sixteen. The image may have been reawakened whilst Lewis was reading a children's story called "The

Pauline Baynes, illustrator of the Narnia books.

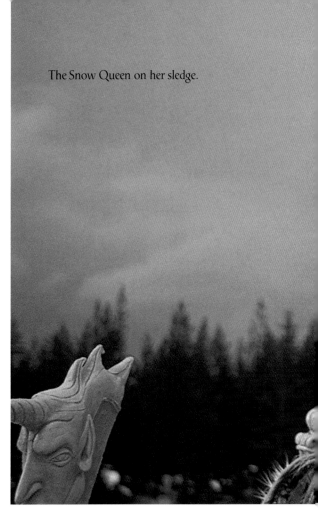

The Snow Queen on her sledge.

Wood that Time Forgot" by one of his former students, Roger Lancelyn Green, who went on to become one of Lewis's biographers and a noted re-teller of myths and legends for children. Another image of Lewis's was of a queen on a sledge, perhaps inspired by Hans Christian Andersen's story *The Snow Queen*.

But it was the image of a lion, recurring in Lewis's dreams—some of them terrifying—that sparked his first Narnia book into life. The lion is a natural symbol of royalty, and in *The Great Divorce* we find wonderful biblical images of lions playing in heaven. Lions are untamable, and all through the books the refrain is "Aslan is not a tame lion." In *The Problem of Pain*, which he had written in 1940, Lewis discusses tame animals, occasioning some controversy as to whether they are better than wild ones. In Narnia he achieves a solution by making some animals talk, which means that they are civilized yet free.

The creation of Aslan was a stroke of genius. It provided the unifying dynamic for the seven books, as well as the focus of spiritual insight and truth-telling. Children are naturally attracted to animal stories. In Aslan we have more than an animal, yet in him are all the factors that can attract children: he is other than grown-ups, yet powerful, more powerful than the witch; he is noble, yet relates to the children with courtesy, so raising them in importance; and yes, he is cuddly, but in a quite profound way of total love and spiritual warmth, again in contrast to the witch, and in a way that includes playfulness and gentleness. And he lays down his life. Lewis's treatment of this in terms of "deep magic" and "a yet deeper magic" is bold and imaginative, and provides genuine tragic dimensions not only for young children, but for all readers who recognize how much evil can be released through human weakness, and how much loving sacrifice is often needed to end it.

The Pevensies

So let us turn to Peter, Susan, Edmund, and Lucy—the Pevensies. Not the average size British middle-class family of the time; not a reflection of Lewis's own family of two boys; but the formula-size family of the "Nesbit tradition," as it has been called, where parents are banished or marginalized, and where the four children (sometimes five with a family pet) act as an autonomous unit for whatever adventures lie in store. Nesbit was writing at the turn of the twentieth century; Enid Blyton continued this type of family adventure story into the 1930s and 1940s, conducting it according to strict formulae, often involving finding buried treasure. One of Nesbit's stories had in fact been called *The Treasure Seekers*, but somewhat in fun.

Lewis structures his family boy, girl, boy, girl, keeping the gender numbers equal, but giving seniority to the male. The setting is contemporary, World War II, when many children in Britain were separated from their parents and evacuated into the country. There is a real enemy in the primary world disrupting the children's lives.

Entering the Secondary World

So the formula is well-known; the entry into a secondary world quickly effected through a magic wardrobe, and in the youngest, Lucy's, footsteps we are quickly taken into the land of talking animals and fauns, dryads and other mythological beings from classical pastoralism. "Furs" become "firs" in a nice dreamplay on words; the tunnel through them is somewhat similar to Alice's falling down the rabbit hole—symbolically the passage through the birth canal into a new world, with a constant, never-extinguished light at the end. But the lamppost is a surprise; one of the images that had sprung from Lewis's unconscious, and which helps give the book its memorability.

The initial scenario of the faun with what looks suspiciously like Christmas shopping appears more similar to *The Wind in the Willows*,

Right: The Pevensie children are entertained to tea. A cozy image from *The Lion, the Witch and the Wardrobe*.

Below: A wooden wardrobe in Lewis's home—perhaps the original "wardrobe."

The Pevensie children emerge from the wardrobe. A scene from the B.B.C. TV adaptation of *The Lion, the Witch and the Wardrobe*.

a comfortable animal bourgeoisie, reinforced by the quintessentially British tea-ceremony—cozy, intimate and safe. We are reminded again of Enid Blyton's concentration on food and meals, especially snug meals with their emphasis on tea, cakes, and other goodies—a concentration Lewis maintains throughout the *Chronicles*, as does Tolkien in *The Hobbit*. Episodes are judged by the availability, or lack, of comfortable British meals.

We notice, too, that there is no language barrier: English is the universal language. We are not in the world of Middle Earth, where interpretation is needed between the common tongue and Elvish (both versions), Orcish, Entish, and so on. Language is no barrier any

The Lion, the Witch and the Wardrobe ends with the four Pevensie children reigning in Narnia. Here they are joined by Aslan.

more than it is in story-reading: we have no sense that Andersen's tales were originally in Danish, Grimm's fairy tales in German, and *Cinderella* in French. All come to us in the common language of story. So with Lewis.

Memorable Episodes

But it is not by such things that we judge the book. It is rather in the memorable images that we have mentioned, and in the memorable episodes. Probably the two most memorable incidents are Edmund's temptation by the Snow Queen/witch, and Aslan's self-sacrifice on the stone table, followed by possibly the most dramatic episode in all the stories, Aslan's glorious resurrection.

Edmund's seduction is the first of many temptation scenes: the witch's in *The Silver Chair*; Jadis's in the garden in *The Magician's Nephew* both directly parallel it. In Edmund's seduction the temptation is to taste and smell, as was Eve's in Milton's depiction in his epic poem *Paradise Lost*, or Tom's temptation to raid the candy cupboard in *The Water Babies* by the Victorian writer Charles Kingsley. Turkish delight (Edmund's temptation) is a particularly cloying, "more-ish" sort of soft candy. Lewis uses it to describe not only the effect of drugs on a user, leaving him or her with the craving for more, but more generally, the reality of "desire" wrongly fulfilled. As we shall see, the concept of desire is central to Lewis. The episode is believable, an accurate description of the false attractiveness of evil; and of how a small temptation can lead to disastrous consequences.

The result of Edmund's "fall," his treachery and betrayal firstly of Lucy then of all the children, leads to the second episode, Aslan's self-sacrifice. It is interesting that many readers, on a first reading, see no immediate parallel with the death of Christ on the cross; there are sufficient differences to keep such an allegorical reading hidden. For example, Aslan's death is on a stone table and by a knife, more akin to Celtic mythology than Biblical narrative. The talk is of "deep magic" and "deeper magic"; the sense that it is only for Edmund that Aslan dies and Aslan negotiates with the witch.

The Lion, the Witch, and the Wardrobe

But on rereading, the parallels become much more insistent. The creator of Narnia has to die to redeem his creation from the hands of evil forces who have already gained control and now a legal right over the world. Specific echoes of Gethsemane and the women weeping at the foot of the cross are heard. Thus, a rereading of *The Lion, the Witch and the Wardrobe* brings out the hidden symbolism. It gives theological expression to the compassion that Lucy particularly feels for Aslan and to her subsequent joy when he comes to life again. An interesting point is that the witch's power is being broken *before* the sacrifice, symbolized in the snow melting, just as Satan's power was being broken from the incarnation of Christ, though it needed his death and resurrection to make permanent the proclamation of the rightful ownership of the kingdom.

The ending of the book sees the four Pevensies reigning in Narnia. The final episode, of their riding out of Narnia back into the wardrobe, leaves more problems than it solves. There is no succession, no other humans appear to be in Narnia, yet it seems necessary for a human to rule. So who will? But this is a problem only a rereading brings up. On the first reading, there is only the shock of finding that no time at all has elapsed in the primary world.

Prince Caspian

Prince Caspian could be seen as a sequel story; it is a "return," and it is located within a year of the Pevensies' first Narnia adventure. Yet, as with the first story, time confusion is immediately obvious. Secondary world time exists almost independently of primary world time (the only thing it doesn't do is go backwards). In Narnia the golden age has passed away; descendants of other "sons of Adam" have invaded and established the kingdom of "New" Narnia. The children are recalled to help the rightful heir to *this* dynasty gain his crown. There are perhaps echoes of English history: the old England of the Anglo-Saxons is replaced by the new kingdom of the Normans. There is no question of going back in history.

Of all the *Chronicles*, *Prince Caspian* is the most pastoral. Lewis celebrates the classical mythology of nature, emphasizing not only its innocence but its spirituality. There is a pastoral dance at the end, just as at the end of his science

Scene from the B.B.C. TV adaptation of *Prince Caspian*. Lewis has sometimes been criticized for his frequent battle scenes.

fiction novel *Voyage to Venus*, which clearly fascinates Lewis, but which probably fascinates children much less. As in *The Lion, the Witch and the Wardrobe*, a battle scene is central to the plot, and probably interests children rather more.

Lewis has sometimes been criticized for the frequent inclusion of such battle scenes, but they are so far remote from modern warfare and the violence of many video games, that this criticism seems barely relevant. Episodes of battle can take on symbolic overtones, as they do in the Bible. Here the battle is resolved in a duel between two fairly incompetent swordsmen, so there is as much comedy as danger. What is unexplained is how the small force of Prince Caspian managed to hold out so long before rescue came at the hands of the Pevensies.

Apart from the duel, the only really memorable and symbolic episode in *Prince Caspian* is Aslan's reappearing (or "epiphany") to Lucy. This becomes a test of her faith and of the others' trust in her. They fail at first, trying to cross a deep gorge by their own efforts. Another theme emerges: the prophetic and the nature of "true" Narnia. In *The Lion, the Witch and the Wardrobe*, the Pevensies are the fulfillment of a long-held prophecy, which, as is typical in a fairystory, comes in verse form. Here, Roonwit, the Centaur, utters prophetic words which need obeying. "Neither Caspian nor the others hesitated for a moment" in their response. The Centaur is the Narnian prophet, as we see later in *The Last Battle*.

As with most sequels, *Prince Caspian* fails to live up to its predecessor. Lewis had not yet quite seen what he could do with Narnia. The book's construction is awkward: Lewis tries to keep two story lines going, that of Caspian and that of the Pevensies, with the two only meeting later in the book. Tone and style suffer in this weak construction. In *The Last Battle* he solves a similar problem by keeping the book within the secondary world, with a single narrative line.

Fantasy Worlds

ONCE THERE WERE four children whose names were Peter, Susan, Edmund, and Lucy.

How easily and simply begins *The Lion, the Witch and the Wardrobe*. Anyone could have written that sentence, certainly any one of the children themselves. It is the "once" that gives it away, though. It means "There weren't really" instead of "there were"; or at least "there were" only in the writer's imagination, and now in our imagination too as readers and viewers. For that is how all storytelling works. The storyteller imagines a world which may or may not be based on the real world he or she—or we—live in; and then tries to get us to live in it while we are reading the book or seeing the film, and perhaps for a little while after, as we talk about the story to others, or think about it or perhaps even write about it.

Imagined Worlds

The storyteller here is C. S. Lewis, who wrote *The Lion, the Witch and the Wardrobe* without perhaps realizing he would have so much to say about his imaginary world that it would need a further six books to tell it all. Lewis's close friend J. R. R. Tolkien was also a storyteller, who invented an even more fully imagined world, which, as we all know, he called Middle Earth. Most people who have read or seen *The Chronicles of Narnia* have also read *The Hobbit* and seen or read *The Lord of the Rings*. Tolkien was particularly interested in the traditional art of storytelling as seen in myths, legends, and fairy stories. He gave an important lecture in 1938 at the University of St. Andrews, Scotland, entitled *On Fairy-Stories*, which was later published, along with a fairy story of his own, as *Tree and Leaf*.

In this lecture he suggests that writers live in two worlds: the primary and the secondary worlds.

Artist's impression of the faun from *The Lion, the Witch and the Wardrobe*.

The writer is actually a subcreator, creating a secondary world in his imagination. In this the writer is quite like God, who created the primary world. That is, for Tolkien, one of the meanings of human is "being created in the image of God."

Sometimes the secondary world is closely based on the real, or primary, world we live in, but not necessarily. When it is quite different we often call the form of writing "fantasy." Science fiction is one form of fantasy, fairy story is another.

It has always been accepted that children enjoy fantasy. In play, younger children "make up" their own little worlds of toys or stuffed animals, or adapt the fantasies they see in comics, on television, or in video games to their own play needs, tastes, and circle of friends. Tolkien's contention is that at one time everyone enjoyed hearing about secondary worlds, when there was no sharp divide between fact and fiction—and it would be a good thing if people returned to this easy, imaginative passage from one world to another, since there is an "imaginative truth" that can be as "true" in its own way as scientific or historical truth.

This idea can be traced back at least as far as the early nineteenth-century Romantic poet Coleridge, whose famous poem *The Rime of the Ancient Mariner* is a powerful "legend of the Fall." Lewis accepted Tolkien's view, and, as we shall see, saw how in creating a secondary world he could present truths about morals, religion, philosophy, and life in general in the real world.

If we think about possible relationships between the two worlds, then we can see that fantasy can take on a number of different forms. For example, Tolkien's fantasy does not refer directly to the primary world—our world—at all. From start to finish it is set in the secondary world, and if humans exist, such as Faramir or Strider, then no connection is made between them and any humans in our world. Ursula Le Guin's *Earthsea* books are

like this, and, to a lesser extent, so are the Harry Potter books. At the other extreme are some of the stories of E. Nesbit, whose children's stories Lewis liked. She often has visitants from a secondary world, such as a Psammead or "sand fairy," who pop into our world and cause all sorts of upsets and mischief to it. Such fantasy can be quite comic, as in parts of Lewis's own *The Magician's Nephew*, where the seven-foot-tall Queen of Charn, Jadis, tried to behave like the tyrant she was in Charn, but merely succeeds in smashing up a hansom cab and a lamppost, and making a smash-and-grab raid on a jeweler's, much to the amusement of the onlookers.

Lewis's Fantasy

But most of Lewis's fantasy, whether the *Chronicles of Narnia* or his science fiction stories, begin in the primary world, and then by some device the main characters are transported into a secondary world where they spend most of the rest of the book. Only at the end do they return to the primary world, where they find hardly any time has passed. Other fantasies like this are *Alice in Wonderland* and *Alice through the Looking-Glass*, where a dream (a very old device) is employed as entry point; and also Madeleine L'Engle's fantasies such as *A Wrinkle in Time*. Sometimes the characters don't want to return, at other times they fear they won't be able to. What is interesting in this sort of fantasy is what entry device the writer will use; how the experiences in the secondary world will change the characters; and how the characters will be able to change the secondary world by their actions, for often they are sent on a quest or mission by some unknown or known force. Nearly all the Narnia stories have such a mission in them, as we shall see. When it is accomplished, the children return "home," though in *The Last Battle* "home" takes on a new meaning.

Reepicheep, the talking mouse, from *The Voyage of the Dawn Treader.*

Judging Fantasy

Before we move on to discuss each of the *Chronicles* in detail, and from there look at the life of C. S. Lewis and his other writings, we will consider how we can judge if a fantasy world has been successfully created. How can we tell if the Narnia stories are really good, beyond our own sense of enjoyment? Of course, you probably would not be starting to read this book if you had not already enjoyed something Lewis wrote, and that enjoyment had made you want to find out more about him and how to understand and appreciate his writings.

Lewis himself suggested three ways of measuring how good a book is. Firstly, as in any story, whether fantasy or not, there is the characterization: do we believe in the characters, do they seem "real"; can we understand how they behave and in some way identify with them, even if they are

talking mice such as Reepicheep in *The Voyage of the Dawn Treader*? Secondly, is the story told in the right tone? This entails respect for the audience. Children especially do not want to be lectured to or talked down to. Nor should the writer talk over their heads, winking, as it were, to the adult behind the child. Despite not having any children of his own at the time of writing *Narnia*, Lewis gets the tone just right. He takes his audience into his confidence, sides with them in matters such as schools and bullying, and at all times respects their integrity. The third test Lewis explains particularly in his book *An Experiment in Criticism*: it is that of rereadability. Can we re-read the text and discover more in it as we do so; and again and again? Or has the text yielded up everything it has the first time around? The present author confesses to having read *The Chronicles of Narnia* at least five times, each time gaining some new insight or pleasure. And his experience is probably typical.

One further test could be suggested. Children are not interested in long descriptions of scenery or characters or in philosophical digressions, yet it is in such ways that many writers for adults convey their deeper meanings. A children's writer needs to use action to do this, symbolically loading individual episodes with whatever meaning he wishes to convey. Such episodes need to be memorable, to resonate in the child's imagination as powerfully as the characters. First-rate children's authors realize this; second-rate ones don't. For second-rate authors, episodes are infinitely interchangeable, and they produce one plot after another according to some predetermined formula. We shall see that in the *Chronicles* each book has its own set of symbolically loaded episodes, quite unique to that book.

The Quests

Much fantasy literature falls into a wider category called "Quest Literature." Typically, a quest is a journey with a mission, where the main characters, or protagonists, are given a set of clues or instructions, since the journey is largely unknown and often one of exploration or discovery. The protagonists are usually tested on this journey, either through temptation or feats that require wisdom and courage. They are often helped on the way, just as they can also be hindered, sometimes supernaturally so in either case.

Quest Literature

The *Chronicles of Narnia* fit to a certain extent into this quest literature. Certainly there is always a sense of mission: even in *The Lion, the Witch and the Wardrobe*, the children come as fulfillment of prophecy, their mission being to reestablish the kingdom and true monarchy. In fact, it is Aslan himself who performs the feats that bring this about, apart from the battle, and it is actually Edmund who hinders him. The other children's brave actions in the battle equalize the equation. In *Prince Caspian*, the mission is again to reestablish the monarchy, but here it is Prince Caspian who rules. The children are helpers rather than protagonists.

The Voyage of the Dawn Treader

In the middle Chronicles, the sense of quest becomes much more emphasized, especially the sense of journey to a destination. Each journey takes a different direction and a different mode of travel. *The Voyage of the Dawn Treader* is a quest by ship to the east, firstly to rediscover the seven lost lords of Narnia, who disappeared on an earlier voyage, but ultimately, to reach the World's End. Here Lewis is perhaps echoing one of his favorite fantasies, William Morris's *The Well at the World's End*. Only the two younger Pevensies are allowed back into Narnia. They take with them quite unwillingly their grim cousin, Eustace, "useless Eustace" as he might be called, a parody of the pupil educated on scientific principles, as was Bitzer in Dickens' novel *Hard Times*. Lewis had called such people "men without chests" in an important earlier essay on education entitled *The Abolition of Man*.

The children rejoin Prince Caspian on board his ship *The Dawn Treader*. There are several memorable episodes in *The Voyage*, for example Eustace's transformation into a dragon, and the final, mysterious myth-laden chapters where they approach the world's edge in a lily-strewn calm and silent sea. Aslan appears in several of these episodes, setting Eustace free and changing him back into the boy he was created to be in a

The Dawn Treader, from the B.B.C. TV adaptation.

regenerative process involving Eustace's repentance for his "dragonish" egotism. Finally Aslan appears as a lamb on the shores of "Aslan's country" before sending them back to the primary world.

The children's entry point into the secondary world is very striking, too: a picture of a sailing ship on the high seas suddenly becomes real and the children fall into it. Such a striking use of a picture as entry point is also to be found in John Masefield's marvelous fantasy, *The Midnight Folk*, written in 1927. Reepicheep, the gallant talking mouse, who made his appearance in *Prince Caspian*, becomes the most interesting of the characters in the *Voyage*.

Despite such memorable episodes and characters, the book is a bit of a mixed bag, going from the sublime to the ridiculous, and with too many literary borrowings. Swift's *Voyage to Laputa*, the third book of *Gulliver's Travels*, seems to provide the literary prototype of sailing from island to island in an episodic and picaresque manner, but Lewis lacks Swift's unity of tone and purpose.

The Silver Chair

If *The Voyage of the Dawn Treader* is a journey east over the sea, then *The Silver Chair* is one northward and underground. In the primary world it begins at Eustace's school; in the secondary, in Aslan's country, which is where the previous novel finished, before Eustace and his friend Jill Pole are transported by air westward to Narnia. The quest is to find the lost heir of Narnia, rather than to reinstate him as in *Prince Caspian*. There is a great feel of fairy story to this tale, and also a feel of the great epic poem Lewis was teaching at the time, the Elizabethan poet Edmund Spenser's *The Fairy Queen*. There are also patterns of temptation, of warnings not heeded, of giants and monsters and knights-at-arms. But there are also strands from boys' adventure stories: Rider Haggard's *She*, Jules Verne's *Journey to the Center of the Earth*, and Swift's *Gulliver's*

Travels, Book 2, where he visits the giants of Brobdignag. And echoes, too, from one of Lewis's favorite authors, George Macdonald, whose *The Princess and the Goblin* is all about underground workings and passages and threats of breakouts by the underground people to capture the kingdom. But the plotline is much stronger than in *The Voyage of the Dawn Treader* and so can fuse together these disparate elements into a single story line.

There are memorable characters and episodes, too. Instead of Reepicheep we have Puddleglum, the lugubrious "marsh-wiggle" to enliven the book. The Lewis's gardener-cum-cook, Paxford, provided the model for him. But it is the temptation scene that proves to be the spiritual center of the book. The queen-witch's temptation of the captive Prince Rillian is not unlike Weston's tempting of the lady in *Perelandra*: it is reductionist and anti-Platonic. Does Narnia really exist or is it only an idealized memory of something else that is quite unprovable and therefore basically a figment of the imagination? The irony of the enchanted captive prince is that he is only being offered his birthright back as a reward for subservience to the witch. Though the two children, Eustace and Jill, have failed three of the four "signs" given them by Aslan at the beginning of the quest, they here manage, with Puddleglum's practical loyalty and commonsense, to come through on the last sign and break the witch's power, which lies in the silver chair.

There are some memorable descriptions, too: the depiction of the northern wastes are vivid, stemming from Lewis's early love of "northernness" and the northern landscape; and also the wonderful opening up of the depths of the earth as the strange underground creatures return to it from the witch's realms. The journey in the secondary world ends where *Prince Caspian* ended, in a

A scene from *The Silver Chair.*

riot of pastoral feasting and dancing. Back in the primary world, Eustace and Jill are now brave enough to face and overcome the school bullies who have been making their lives such a misery.

The Horse and His Boy

The Horse and his Boy is also about the finding of a lost heir, though this is not the quest. It takes us back to Old Narnia, but this time there are no earth children involved, though it is during the Pevensies' reign. It is set entirely in the secondary world, in fact, and involves a journey from the south by horseback, over the deserts of Calormen. The quest is initially that of a talking horse, Bree, who has been kidnapped in his youth from Narnia and wishes to return there, but needs to have a rider to avoid suspicion. This is the boy Shasta, who turns out to be the lost twin prince of Archenland and its rightful heir. This is a classic Romance plot motif to be found, for example, in many of Shakespeare's romance comedies, such as *Twelfth Night*.

A lot is made again of "free" Narnia, rather than "old" or "new." Aslan intervenes frequently to guide the characters, whereas in *The Silver Chair* he had given them signs but not epiphanies or appearances. It is much more a story as sheer story with a Romance happy meeting at the end. There are few remarkable or symbolic episodes; the pace of the story as both quest and pursuit carry the reader forward. The talking horses, Shasta and his lady mare Bree, and their relationship with the two very contrasting child riders provide interesting dialogue and perspectives on behavior. As in most Romance, true noble blood will manifest itself and Shasta's bravery is shown to be inborn despite his ignoble upbringing, in contrast to the three other characters' more obviously noble status.

The Magician's Nephew

The last two *Chronicles* form the two slices of bread round the sandwich filling of the five books we have been discussing. In *The Magician's Nephew* Lewis explains the origins of Narnia and some of its strange features: talking animals, the presence of evil, and the ever-shining lamppost in Lantern Waste. It is set in the England of E. Nesbit, at the turn of the nineteenth and twentieth centuries. The human interest focuses on Digory's mother dying: can she be healed? The mythic interest lies in the contrast of dying and newly born worlds, Charn and Narnia. They parallel the two planets of Lewis's earlier science fiction trilogy, Malacandra and Perelandra in *Out of the Silent Planet* and *Voyage to Venus* respectively. But unlike Malacandra, the dying world of Charn is totally evil, as is Jadis, its witch-empress. She finds her way, through the two children, Digory and Polly, into the world of Narnia just as Aslan is creating it.

Thus evil seems tragically to spoil this pristine world right from the start. Some of the tragic overtones are made farcical in the figure of Uncle Andrew, the magician who has unwittingly released a great force of evil. The others are contained by Digory's ability to resist the temptation of the fruit offered him by Jadis, in a rerun of Eve's temptation in the Garden of Eden. His resistance not only keeps out the evil, though it is not defeated; it also becomes a means of redemption. He is able to carry an apple from the tree that miraculously grows from the gathered fruit back to the primary world to heal his mother.

Themes of life, creation, and dying are thus laid out. The depiction of Charn has a prophetic note: at the time when Lewis was writing, the possibility of worldwide nuclear catastrophe was just being recognized. Such power is symbolized in the "forbidden word" which finally brings Charn's destruction. And as with the previous books, there are quests: Uncle Andrew's evil quest to Digory, which is overtaken by Aslan's. Here the quest is to the east, by flying horse this time, a similar direction to that taken in *The Last Battle*, which also describes the garden lying to the west of

Some of the major characters from *The Lion, the Witch and the Wardrobe*.

Narnia. Such a western garden is to be found in the Greek myth of the Garden of the Hesperides, whereas in the Biblical account, Eden lies to the east. Similarly in Lewis's allegorical *The Pilgrim's Regress*, John travels westward, though his original vision of a magic island was in the east. In the end, of course, west meets east.

The structure of *The Magician's Nephew* allows much more travel between the primary and the secondary world. There are episodes which form powerful images: the rows of past monarchs in the halls of Charn; the world between the worlds; the marvelous creation of Narnia through Aslan's singing, similar to the opening creation scenes of Tolkien's *Silmarillion*. And as the book is reread, so certain themes stand out: the choice of certain creatures to be talking animals; the unity of creation; the democratic nature of the monarchy set up; the pettiness of evil. But perhaps *The Magician's Nephew* is just too ambitious and tries to say too much, so that ultimately nothing is said quite clearly enough.

The Last Battle

This cannot be said for *The Last Battle*, which was awarded the Carnegie Medal, a prestigious British award for the best children's book of the year. It has been argued that the medal was really awarded for the whole series; but it could just as well be argued that this is the best book of all the *Chronicles* and achieves a stature that the others do not quite attain. If you have read it once, it is almost unbearably sad to read it again. It is a painful, threatening book, because good seems so easily defeated; Narnia is tricked out of its heritage; and the false god Tash, seen for the first time properly in *The Horse and his Boy*, literally comes to Narnia to assume demonic power.

The strength of evil, so well portrayed in *That Hideous Strength*, is simply and starkly shown, as is human (and dwarvish) cunning and treachery. Yet the moment of defeat—at a stable door significantly—becomes the moment of Aslan's judgement. The book suddenly takes on endtime dimensions, as the end of Narnia comes suddenly upon us. And then, out of the misery, the revelation of a "truer" Narnia is shown us, "higher up and further in," and the perfect forms of Platonism become fused with the Paradise of a "new heavens and a new earth."

It comes as a shock to realize that the end of Narnia for the children is also the end of their earthly life, for they have been killed in the primary world in a rail crash. So the end of the book really does take us up to heaven itself, where primary and secondary worlds meld. Eternal life is seen as a story, too, and "now at last they were beginning chapter one of the great story." This is an incredibly bold stroke for what has often been a very safe world of writing (that is, for children). It is amazing that what starts with something so petty and miserable can finish on such a glorious and powerful note.

The Last Battle in a sense becomes a re-reading of all the *Chronicles*; every character except Susan reappears and the "true" Narnia is fully revealed in the context of eternity. And it is structured differently: we are told at once that we are "in the last days of Narnia." There is a sense of tragedy, not of quest or mission. Past motifs are no longer comic. The summoning of Eustace and Jill does little to help; the inevitable battle is doomed to failure. Episodes are memorable because they are shocking: the black dwarves shooting the talking horses; the appearance of the demon Tash; the cunning manipulation in the night scenes, akin to George Orwell's *Animal Farm*.

We inevitably ask the question: Why kill Narnia off? Why kill the children off? It takes several rereadings to establish all the answers. At one level, clearly, Lewis felt he had no more stories to write. Some series can go on endlessly, but most good writers know when their true creativity has ceased. *The Last Battle*

is the last as well as the best. What more could be said?

But this is too reductionist an answer. We need to look more deeply, to the biblical witness to a "Last Day," to a last battle; to a judgement; to a new earth, and therefore a new Narnia. This ties in with Lewis's Platonism, which sees everything on earth as a copy of an ideal form in heaven. This philosophy released Lewis's imagination, as we see the "perfect" Narnia appear at the end, a much more intensely experienced reality. Heaven is not some shadowy afterlife, but a

Artist's impression of the creatures killing Aslan.

far more solid reality than earth: it is our earthly life that is the "Shadow Land."

Lastly, death itself is a reality, one not to be feared by those who believe. In Lewis's day, children's literature tended to avoid such a topic, though Ursula Le Guin deals well with the fear of death in the third of her *Earthsea* books. By taking us into the afterlife, Lewis seeks to overcome our natural fear and our puzzlement about a final judgement. It is a tremendously bold move, but Lewis had prepared himself to make it in much of his earlier Christian writing.

Allegory or Fantasy?

We should consider what Lewis was actually doing in creating this imaginative world, and define the readers he intended. Was it for children that he wrote, and was it to teach them valuable truths about Christianity?

We usually call literature that sets out to teach in a systematic way didactic. One type of didactic writing is allegory, such as Lewis's *The Pilgrim's Regress*, or its greater predecessor, Bunyan's *The Pilgrim's Progress*. In his allegory,

Lewis shows not only how he came to faith, but what is false about each of the beliefs and attitudes he encountered on the way. However, when giving a talk on the *Chronicles of Narnia* to the Library Association in 1952, entitled "On Three Ways of Writing for Children," Lewis rejects any didactic purpose for the *Chronicles*. Rather he wanted a form of literature where he could leave things out, to check the "expository demon in me."

At most we could say that where Lewis echoes allegorical writers such as Bunyan, Spenser, or Swift, then his stories do take on allegorical possibilities. For example, one popular device in allegory is the journey (paralleling our journey through life), and in *The Voyage of the Dawn Treader* some of the incidents *could* be interpreted allegorically; as could *The Horse and his Boy* be seen to parallel Lewis's own spiritual journey. But the books do not need to be read like this at all, whereas with true allegory, they would have to be to make sense.

Lewis's Purposes

If Lewis's purposes were not didactic or allegorical, what were they? He himself suggests three reasons for choosing the form of children's fantasy as his medium. Firstly, he felt it was the best medium to say what he wanted. He didn't write specifically *for* children, he claims; it was the *form* of fiction he went for. In fact he argues that the best children's books are those which everyone can read, whatever their age. Secondly, if he is writing for anyone, it is for himself—"what I still like reading now that I am in my fifties." Thirdly, there is the "past watchful dragons" principle—a phrase taken from another essay, "Sometimes Fairy Stories May Say Best What's to be Said." By "past watchful dragons" Lewis means that children are often on their guard against anything "religious," since to them it means they are supposed to feel things they actually don't (something Lewis himself experienced over prayer as a boy).

Lewis believed fantasy is the best way to make children experience in a real way such spiritual realities as the holy, joy, our own sinfulness, and love for a divine being in living form.

Myth and Fantasy

Lewis derives fantasy from myth, and as we shall see, for him myth appeals directly to our imaginations, and releases powerful feelings which cannot necessarily be expressed intellectually. But because these can be so powerful, Christians often fear fantasy, since its misuse could be so serious. We see this misuse today in the connection of fantasy with the occult, for example. Lewis himself clearly saw these dangers, as he saw the dangers of Romanticism. Weston's tempting arguments in *Voyage to Venus*, where he talks of "the force," are not far removed from some recent popular science fiction films.

But as Lewis discovered in the nineteenth-century Scots author George MacDonald's writing, fantasy can also be used properly for good. His understanding of the psychology of C. G. Jung's archetypes helped him to see the emotional importance of fantasy; the theology of fantasy was worked out in discussion with the Inklings and incorporated into Tolkien's essay *On Fairy-Stories*. A true creation will parallel the unseen spiritual world that Christianity asserts, and will cause our spirits to reach out in longing for reality.

Christian Insights

Lewis said that when he first started writing about Narnia, Christianity was not even intended: "It pushed itself in of its own accord." So we could say that while there is nothing systematic, there is an imaginative expression of Christian truths, which could bring insights to readers, whether children or not. But in the freedom of interpretation of myth, these insights need not necessarily be apprehended as such, or in the same way by everyone. The main expressions of religious themes might be seen as:

1. Aslan's death and resurrection (though it is not a "for everyone" substitutionary death, like that of Jesus).
2. Aslan's royalty ("the lion of the tribe of Judah").
3. The creation of the world and the entry of evil into it.
4. The final judgement and the Last Day, with new heavens and a new earth.
5. The nature of time (one day as a thousand with God).
6. Election (some animals are chosen to be talking animals; the children are called into Narnia for a purpose).
7. Revelation (Aslan shows himself from time to time) and prophecy.

This is very close to what Lewis wrote once to a young correspondent: "Suppose there were a world like Narnia, and it needed saving, and the Son of God went to redeem, as He came to redeem. What might it, in that world, all have been like?" (*Letters to Children*). Lewis in the letter then goes on to list very similar points to the above.

We need perhaps to see, though, that certain important Christian truths are not expressed. For example:

1. There is little sense of incarnation (Aslan doesn't *become* a lion).
2. There is little sense of the Fatherhood of God.
3. The Holy Spirit is vague—Aslan does no more than breathe on the children in *The Silver Chair*; there is no personal devil.
4. There is no religious practice, no church, no worship.

The same omissions can be said of Tolkien's fantasies, though he too was a practicing Christian. Some of these concepts are notoriously difficult to express as fantasy or allegory at all. These omissions should act, if nothing else does, as a warning against over-systematizing. Lewis's point is that one world is not like another; it must have enough in it of our world for us to see parallels and gain insights or take warnings, especially in terms of moral behavior and choices; but the differences need to be there, exciting our wonder and increasing our longing for "deep heaven."

Violent and Anti-Female?

In this battle for meaning Lewis has been criticized on political and gender grounds. It has been suggested, for example, that Lewis is reactionary, obsessed with violence, abandons the concept of personal responsibility, and is male centered. As evidence of the last, his depiction of evil as largely feminized, from Jadis, to the snow queen, to the enchantress or Lamia of *The Silver Chair* is cited. The object of such female wiles are mainly boys: Edmund succumbing, Digory resisting. In defense it can be said that the evil in *The Last Battle* is entirely male; if Aslan is male, so is Tash. And although Uncle Andrew and Miraz (in *Prince Caspian*) are parody sources of evil, the parody cunning of the ape in *The Last Battle* is just as serious as the *real* evil of the Calormenes. Susan's absence from the final reconciliation through her loss of faith is also cited as evidence of Lewis's anti-female bias. Her loss of faith does seem trivial: she has reached a typical adolescent false sophistication and demotes belief in Narnia to childish games. The loss of faith is poignantly felt; she is no Judas figure. But it does happen in real life. And she is counterbalanced by her sister Lucy, whose intuitive faith means that Aslan is able to reveal himself to her more easily than to anyone else.

In terms of being a political reactionary, it must be said that Lewis's monarchy in Narnia (as opposed to Charn or Calormen) is extremely democratic. A council of talking animals is formed to help the very working-class first King and Queen of Narnia. The exercise of government is almost nonexistent: a pastoral egalitarianism seems to be the preferred politics of Narnia. In fact, it is the absence of government in *The Last Battle* that causes the takeover of evil to be so easy. Lewis is showing the dangers of political anarchy on the one hand, and of fascism, the Calormene state, on the other. Tolkien shows a similar rural democracy in the Shire. Lewis has a keen sense of the corrupting nature of power, something that anyone living through the mid-twentieth century was keenly aware of.

In terms of other modern concerns, the description of the Calormenes might be seen as racist, a parody portrayal of an Arab-type culture. On the other hand, Lewis has a keen sense of the unity of nature and the need for ecological balance. The moral worth of characters are usually judged, in fact, by their attitude to trees: evil men fear them and seek to destroy them or avoid the forests; good men plant and nurture them. In this Tolkien and Lewis stand together with modern day conservationists. Obviously current concerns change over time. What is remarkable is that Lewis's religious and Romantic beliefs, as expressed in the *Chronicles of Narnia*, generate such deep and lasting truths that his work is able to stay in touch with such concerns. But to understand these religious and Romantic beliefs more fully, we need to turn back to the beginning of his life and trace his development.

Lewis's Beginnings

Below: C. S. Lewis as a young boy.

". . . it is like nothing so much as the assembly of white foam caps when a fresh breeze is on a summer sea. And the roads are white too; there is no tarmac yet. . . . the whole country is a turbulent democracy of little hills. . . . not your hard English sunlight; make it paler, make it softer . . . deepening it. . . . And beyond all this, so remote that they seem fantastically abrupt . . . imagine the mountains."

An Ulster Childhood

This is the lyrical description Clive Staples Lewis gives to his birthplace, county Down in Northern Ireland. It comes from his autobiography *Surprised by Joy*, but it could have been from several of his letters, such was the abiding impression of Ulster on him. During his boyhood there, in the first years of the twentieth century, Northern Ireland did not exist as a political entity, as it does now, and so the region did not have the sad overtones of violence and division that it does for us today. The term "Ulster" meant for Lewis a beautiful area in a beautiful country, with a past that was more romantic than turbulent. Indeed, it has been

suggested that if his invented land of Narnia is based on anything, it must be on the countryside of Ireland.

Lewis was born in 1898 in Belfast, not perhaps the most romantic of cities, but before he was very old, his parents had moved to what were then the outskirts, to a suburb called Strandtown. This was within walking and easy cycling distance of the countryside of county Down. Although he left home quite early to go to boarding school, and only returned for comparatively brief stays during his youth, C. S. Lewis remained closely in touch with the area all his life. Just before his death, he was planning another of the summer holidays in Ireland that were his custom, especially with his boyhood friend, Arthur Greeves. Although Lewis grew to love the English countryside too, his first impressions of England were very unfavorable. Writing from school in Malvern (which to many people is the epitome of England's beauty), he says to Arthur:

C. S. Lewis on a cycle trip with his brother Warren.

"It makes me furious to think of your being able to walk about your house and ours and all the beautiful places we know in the country while I am cooped up in this hot, ugly country of England. . . . County Down must be looking glorious now. . . . The sunrise over the Holywood Hills, and the fresh stillness of the early morning are well worth the trouble of early rising. . . ."

One of the features he clearly missed was the sea. "I cannot bear to live too far away from it," he writes. In fact he spent most of his life well away from it, at Oxford; but Narnia is certainly full of the sea.

Although Ulster is not just a place, but a culture, and one that is often stigmatized as narrowly, even fanatically, religious, C. S. Lewis was never affected by this side of it. He tells Arthur Greeves in later life that he is neither attracted nor repelled by the "Puritanism" he sees there. We may say without doubt that for Lewis, Ulster was a positive source of life and beauty, which was for him always universal and never provincial.

The Lewis family

The Lewises had only been Ulstermen for three generations—a relatively short time when compared with some of the Protestant families, such as the Hamiltons, his mother's side, who had settled there from Scotland in the reign of King James I and had at some stage become allied with even older Anglo-Irish blood. His mother's family touched on the Irish upper class and many had become clergy, and one a bishop.

By contrast, the Lewises were working-class people from the Wrexham area of North Wales. Grandfather Richard Lewis had emigrated to Ulster and done well in ship-building, showing considerable intelligence. His son Albert, Lewis's father, received a good education at Lurgan College, became a solicitor and married Florence Hamilton in 1894. She was a brilliant mathematician, having graduated from Queen's College,

Belfast, in 1885 with a first-class degree in logic and a second in mathematics. Their two sons were born in 1895 and 1898.

In *Surprised by Joy*, Lewis characterizes the two sides of the family emotionally: his father's Welsh side he sees as melancholic, very up-and-down and liable to unhappiness; whereas his mother's side was settled, happy and affectionate, critical and ironic. He certainly seems to have reacted against his father in a number of ways. Albert Lewis's intense absorption in politics left his son indifferent to them all his life; his father's overt emotionalism left C. S. Lewis afraid of outward displays of feelings. Always, too, he speaks of a fear of paternal abandonment, perhaps partly created by the early loss of his mother in August 1908, which also caused his

father to retire into a personal grief, unable to carry his two sons' loss.

Such circumstances made C. S. Lewis's relationship with his elder brother Warren ("Warnie", as he was always known, Lewis being known as "Jack") very important to him. There was never any obvious sibling rivalry between them. Throughout their life they cooperated closely together, and for a while, after his retirement from an army career, Warren acted as Jack's secretary and the family historian. The brothers' closeness as boys, if anything, withdrew them further from their father.

After his father died in 1929, Lewis wrote: "When I saw the affection between them [a colleague and his father] . . . and then remembered how abominably I had treated

C. S. Lewis and Warren with their father Albert.

my father . . . I was humiliated." But his father must bear much of the blame, we feel. As his sons grew up he forced an unnatural closeness on them, allowed them no privacy, and yet refused to visit them in England. No boys could be expected to make sense of such conflicting messages.

Prep School

After his father's death, Jack Lewis followed in Warren's footsteps to boarding school in England. It takes six chapters of Lewis's autobiographical *Surprised by Joy* to describe the trauma of his four schools, all of which were part of the British public school system or the prep schools that fed them. When we think that this book was written some forty years after these episodes, we are amazed at the anger and outrage that shrinks the time span. We feel Lewis is having to exorcise some deep evil he senses still lodged within his spirit.

Lewis's father clearly had little idea what the system was like, or how to make informed choices within it. Warren seems to have been more outgoing and resilient than his younger brother, and more able to suppress his own unhappiness, and so the father can perhaps be forgiven for not immediately spotting the damage that was being done. So bad, though, was the first prep school (or "concentration camp" as Lewis called it) that it was closed soon afterward and the headmaster declared insane.

After a term at a local public school in Belfast itself, Lewis spent two years at a much better prep school in Malvern, Cherbourg School (now a girls' school, Ellerslie), while his brother attended Malvern College. "Much better" is relative, of course, since it was here that he lost both what little Christian faith he had and his innocence (Lewis gives no details). On his own admission he became vulgar and snobbish. It is a fairly consistent feature of his writings that schools come out badly, for instance in the Narnia chronicles and in *The Abolition of Man*.

Malvern College

Lewis's greatest criticism is reserved for Malvern College, however perhaps because he had high hopes for it. In *Surprised by Joy* it is called "Wyvern." His brother had just left when Lewis arrived in 1913. He describes it as being run by an in-group of socially-privileged boys called "The Bloods." The school staff seemed to have little control of anything but the academic side, homosexuality was rife, and so was the cult of the physical. Learning of any sort was looked down on, though the school possessed an excellent library, which Lewis used when he could get away from the meaningless chores thrust on him by older boys.

The only mitigation to Lewis's anger comes when he considers that most of the "Bloods" were killed in World War I. His attitude to their deaths is ambivalent; but clearly he does not see them as the flower of Britain's youth, as contemporary English poets did. Indeed, a strong dislike of all public school types of patriotism and imperialism manifests itself in his writings, and can probably be traced back to this period. It has been suggested, even by Warren, that Malvern was no worse than other schools of its sort—an argument which could be taken to mean they were all equally as bad, which seems unlikely. What it clearly shows is that Lewis received an education despite his schooling, not because of it.

One of the redeeming features of this time was the beginnings of Lewis's friendship with Arthur Greeves, to whom Jack once wrote: "You so often share feelings of mine which I cannot explain." Arthur had lived near the Lewises in Belfast, but it was only by chance one vacation that Lewis suddenly discovered a similarity with Arthur, not only in their love of books, reading, and mythology, but also in the quality of their spiritual appetites. Arthur was from a Plymouth Brethren family, of independent means, but suffered poor health, which meant he was, unlike Lewis, if anything, overprotected. He received some train-

Lewis's dormitory at Malvern College.

ing at the Slade School of Art in London, and exhibited a few times. The companionship that sprang up more than compensated for Warren's departure to Sandhurst to become an army officer, and it proved to be lifelong. Lewis's letters to Arthur, to be found in the book *They Stand Together*, give a fascinating insight into his spiritual and intellectual journey through life.

Private Tutoring

In the end Lewis wrote to his father asking to be taken away from Malvern. Fortunately his father responded, and then did the best thing possible: he sent Lewis for private tutoring to his old headmaster at Lurgan College, W. T. Kirkpatrick, or "The Great Knock," as he was nicknamed. Although he had retired to Bookham in Surrey by this time, Kirkpatrick's intellectual vigor and strength of character,

which had made him such an able headmaster (he became head at the age of only thirty) remained undimmed. His impression on Lewis was profound and long-lasting, especially his totally logical approach to life. Although he clearly imparted much learning to Lewis, especially in the classics and to a lesser extent in modern languages, it was his quality of mind that Lewis really took to and imbibed. Every statement had to be justified; every case clearly argued.

Lewis took to the new regime of study, dialectic (reasoning) and leisure pursuits like a duck to water. He told Arthur he had never been happier in his life. He had time to read much English literature, though Kirkpatrick never supervised nor discussed this with him, and started to enjoy walking in the countryside of southern England. By living with Kirkpatrick and his wife in a settled domestic situation, he gained some emotional stability. The collapse of domestic life he had experienced at his mother's death was now, in an unacknowledged way, being put back together. In all, he spent two years with the Kirkpatricks, showing exceptional promise as a student, and developing habits of thinking, working, and living that stayed with him the rest of his life.

C. S. Lewis as a young man.

Trenches and Spires

Kirkpatrick wrote to Lewis's father that he could be a writer or a scholar "but you'll not make anything else of him." Lewis himself realized this. The natural next step therefore seemed to be to try for a scholarship to one of the Oxford colleges, so in the winter of 1916 Lewis traveled up to sit the necessary exams. Thus began an association with Oxford that lasted the rest of his life.

Lewis recalls his first entry into the city as being rather bizarre, for he took the wrong turn out of the railway station and started walking out of the city through its suburbs. Then he turned around. "There, behind me, far away, never more beautiful since, was the fabled cluster of spires and towers." He was duly awarded a scholarship at University College, one of the oldest of the Oxford colleges. He went up the next year, soon enlisting as an officer cadet.

Lewis did not have to enlist, since the Irish were exempt from compulsory military service. However, he had already decided that it was his duty, even though, as he told Arthur at the time, "I do not usually take much interest in the war." He remained at Oxford until commissioned as second lieutenant in the Somerset Light Infantry. He received several postings before arriving at the front line on his nineteenth birthday in November 1917.

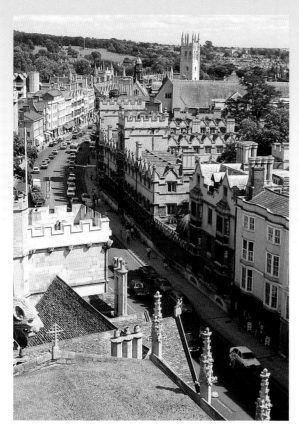

The High Street, Oxford.

By this stage of the war everyone knew how terrible trench conditions were; the earlier death-or-glory attitudes had largely evaporated. Lewis's attitude was stoical: he had expected it to be awful (unlike when he went to Malvern) and it was awful. His letters to Arthur at the time hardly mention actual conditions, but discuss the books he was somehow managing to read. In *Surprised by Joy* he briefly mentions soldierly comradeship and some of the horrors; but he felt he experienced them as if he were someone else. He caught trench fever, and then on his return to the front line was lightly wounded in April 1918.

Oxford Again

C. S. Lewis was demobbed in January 1919, and resumed his studies at Oxford. He tells us very little about these in his autobiography, preferring to describe the patterns of his thinking and the many new and exciting

Magdalen College, Oxford.

The Kilns, Headington, home of Lewis for many years.

friends he made at Oxford, some of whom, such as Owen Barfield, were crucial and lifelong. The first part of his degree was in Greek and Latin; the second in philosophy.

Lewis graduated with a double first, but competition for teaching and tutorial posts or "fellowships," was so fierce that Lewis was advised to get "another arrow to his bow" by studying a third course. English language and literature was a growth area at the time, and this fitted in well with his own enthusiasm for the subject. It meant taking a three-year course in one year, including the learning of Old English (or Anglo-Saxon). He succeeded, adding a third first degree, a remarkable achievement, since he had had no formal academic training in English until that time.

Lewis's difficulty now remained to obtain a university teaching post. His father willingly continued to support him financially while Lewis applied for one post after another, especially in the field of philosophy, in which he finally obtained a temporary appointment.

His first lecture was attended by four students! Then in 1925 C. S. Lewis applied, without much hope, for an English fellowship at Magdalen College. He was successful. This brought him a secure teaching post, rooms in college, and a reasonably generous income.

This time his first lecture overflowed with students and he had to look for a larger lecture theatre. Thus began one of the most distinguished English university teaching careers of the twentieth century.

"Home"

As an officer cadet, Lewis had made friends with a fellow Irish student, Patrick Moore. Moore's mother had separated from her husband, and she came to be near Patrick with her daughter, Maureen. Lewis and Patrick promised each other that if either of them were to be killed in the war, the survivor would look after the other's parent. Lewis took this promise extraordinarily seriously, even before Patrick's death in the front line.

It is not possible to discover Lewis's exact sentiments toward Mrs. Moore, since he refused to discuss them in *Surprised by Joy* or at any other time. We find the clearest hints in his letters to Arthur perhaps; since he did not want his father to know about his close involvement with Mrs. Moore, Arthur was the only person he could tell anything to. Certainly when Arthur first wrote to Mrs. Moore, Lewis told him he was so glad that "the two people who matter most to me are in touch."

Another letter to Arthur, describing a typical undergraduate day, is also revealing: after morning lectures he cycles out to Mrs. Moore's at "our own hired house," staying there to work until eleven o'clock in the evening, when he returns to college. After his first, compulsory, year in college he shared a home with Mrs. Moore until her death. They lived first in lodgings, and then, when his father died in 1929, leaving Warren and Jack Lewis sufficient money to buy a property, in a house on Headington Quarry, called "The Kilns." Warren joined them there after he retired from the army in the 1930s. Maureen Moore moved away in 1940 when she married.

Mrs. Moore

By all accounts, living with Mrs. Moore was not easy—she gave Lewis continuous domestic chores to do; she seems to have had no intellectual capacity; and she complained a great deal about her health. It is hardly surprising that Lewis owns to having to wrestle with irritability and bad-temper in his domestic life. Perhaps the convert's mother in *The Screwtape Letters* owes something to her. Warren clearly thought she was silly, yet continued to live at The Kilns. Others, such as Barfield and the neighbors, liked her, Barfield describing her as a "generous and tireless hostess."

Although we could explain this continuing relationship in terms of an excessive sense of duty on Lewis's part toward his dead friend, it would seem more probable that Mrs. Moore provided the parenting that Lewis desperately lacked, and a stable home from which he could live his life. (The writer A. N. Wilson argues that Lewis and Mrs. Moore had a sexual relationship.) Even when he had rooms in Magdalen, he would still walk out to The Kilns every afternoon, and live there during the vacation. More tellingly, perhaps, he always called where she was "home" and "the family," and referred to her as "my mother," especially later when she became ill. Mrs. Moore was bedridden from 1944, after a stroke, and died in 1951.

The Kilns itself, Lewis's home from 1930 to his death, lay in an eight-acre garden and "is such stuff as dreams are made on," as Lewis quoted when he moved in. It was private and secluded then, with woods, a cliff, and a small lake or bathing pool. Nowadays there is much more building around it, and a conference center has been built on the site.

Surprised by Joy

Right: Magdalen College Chapel, Oxford.

IN OUTLINING SOME OF THE features of the early world of C. S. Lewis, we have mentioned several times his autobiography *Surprised by Joy,* first published in 1955. This is a special sort of autobiography, not concentrating on the events of his life, but tracing his spiritual journey to Christianity. In fact, there is a much earlier book, *The Pilgrim's Regress,* published only a few years after his conversion, in 1933, which also traces a spiritual journey, in a more allegorical form. It is not so directly autobiographical, but clearly its hero, John, is Lewis himself. This has never been such a popular book as *Surprised by Joy,* partly because we are not used to allegory, and partly because there is a good deal of philosophical debate in it. Lewis himself never again attempted such a straightforward allegory, even though one of his specializations was medieval allegory, and he thoroughly understood how it worked.

Hints of Heaven

Before we try to trace his spiritual journey to faith, we need to establish certain key concepts in Lewis's writing and thought, the first of which is "Desire," and its relationship with the "Joy" of the title of the autobiography. The first thing to realize about C. S. Lewis is that beneath the intellectual scholar and philosopher, there was a powerful romantic, although he kept this part of himself very private until the time of his conversion, when slowly the two elements became more integrated and public.

The first section of *The Pilgrim's Regress* opens with John experiencing as a boy the law as institutional religion represented it. But his next experience, which feels like an emotional explosion, is a vision of a far island, and a tremendous longing for it. It is this longing or "desire" that sets him off on his journey, much of which is spent in meeting people who either dismiss this longing and its object, or suggest false paths toward it. This is essentially the pattern that Lewis fills out in his autobiography. In the crucial first chapter he compares his earliest impressions of his parents' interests—politics, for example, and logical argument—with an innate romanticism on his part, "the horns of elfland" as he calls them.

He then describes certain experiences as a child. He says of these "in a sense the central story of my life is about nothing else." The first was a memory of a little moss garden his brother had made: "It is difficult to find words strong enough for the sensation which came over me. . . . it was a sensation, of course, of desire; but for what? . . . It had taken only a moment of time; and in a certain sense everything else that had ever happened to me was insignificant in comparison. "

The other experiences arose from literature, but were of similar intensity. The object of desire could not be located, though

part of the desire was to reexperience the sensation. So the experience was both pleasurable, and therefore joyful, and yet painful, in that it left him wanting more. He continued to experience such magic moments as a child, and then they stopped, and indeed were forgotten about, when he went to school. He calls this period "The Dark Ages," to be followed quite suddenly by a "reconversion" experience, bringing in the "Renaissance" while at Malvern.

From then on he knew such desire and joy from time to time, usually connected at first with the Norse and Germanic myths and legends which had reawakened the sensation. He found, however, he could not control its coming or going; he also discovered how different it was from pleasure, or sexuality, or the occult. The nearest experiences he read about were in the Romantic poets, in which he quickly became immersed. He finally realized two things: first, that joy was Desire, and "our wantings are our best havings" as he wrote to a friend; and secondly, the memory of past moments of Joy/Desire were, in fact, further experiences of Desire.

It is significant that in his book *The Problem of Pain* it is in the chapter on heaven that Lewis universalizes these experiences and puts them into their fullest Christian context. Ultimately the desire is for heaven itself, which is our soul's home; and he assumes that everyone has such moments of immortal longing: "All the things that have ever deeply possessed your soul have been but hints of it [heaven]." It was the search for the object of this desire that finally drove toward faith

Shadows of Reality

We have just mentioned the Norse Germanic mythologies which reawakened in him the deep sensations of joy and desire. Lewis talks of "pure northernness" engulfing him, and it was the discovery that Arthur Greeves shared that "northernness" that bonded them together as youths. "Myth" is another central concept we need to examine. We use the term in its literary sense of stories which seek to explain the mysteries of life, birth, death, rebirth and the seasonal cycles, origins, and creation and which center around gods or demigods, legendary heroes.

Lewis's early feeling for myth, whether Norse or Germanic, as at first, or Celtic, Greek, or Roman, later, was emotional and spiritual. There was no thought in his mind that they might be true, let alone historical. In this he was probably like most people who see myth as untrue stories, however beautiful, which we distinguish from reality.

Certainly, Lewis owns up to a sort of schizophrenia as a youth and young man: with his heart, clinging to what myth gave him; with his mind, completely rejecting any sort of truth or reality it might have. It was the realization that myth might after all be true that finally led him to a complete acceptance of Christianity. He wrote to Arthur in September 1931 that he had had "a good long satisfying talk in which I learned a lot" with two Christian friends, about metaphor, myth, and Christianity. He does not record this conversation in *Surprised by Joy*, but a significant reference to the dialogue appears in *The Pilgrim's Regress*, where John finds himself suddenly praying to God to translate "our halting metaphor" into his "great, unbroken speech." This refers to something that is mentioned in the autobiography: Lewis's shock when an atheist friend suddenly blurted out, "Rum thing, all that . . . about the Dying God. It looks as if it had really happened once."

Myth Becomes Fact

Certainly this is the line that Lewis took from then on. In both *Miracles* and *The Problem of Pain* he takes a footnote to explain myth as something which could have occurred. But the real marrying of his old and his new attitudes is perhaps most clearly set out in his essay

Satan resting on the mountains as illustrated by Doré for Milton's *Paradise Lost*.

Romantic revolution at the turn of the eighteenth and nineteenth centuries, which included poets such as William Wordsworth, S. T. Coleridge and John Keats. Their romanticism had two main "witnesses": the power of the imagination to shape truth, and a love for nature. Lewis, too, sees the imagination (not the mind) as the primary organ for the reception of truth—hence the power of myth, since it speaks straight to the imagination.

Plato and Christianity

His love of nature is recounted in his autobiography, coming from experiences of joy, and acting as a reminder of it. The philosophic bedrock of his Romanticism was Platonism. Although Plato was a Greek philosopher, there have always been strands of Christianity which have been able to absorb Platonism without difficulty, including two of the English writers Lewis admired most, Edmund Spenser and John Milton. At an imaginative level, Lewis had perhaps always been a Platonist: the sense that the glimpses we have of joy are gleams of a much greater, otherworldly reality, for which our soul longs and yearns, is pure Platonism, and is to be found in Thomas Traherne and William Wordsworth, two poets whom Lewis acknowledges.

Lewis's becoming a Christian "baptized" this Platonism and gave it intellectual coherence, a process which is set out quite explicitly in *The Pilgrim's Regress*, where the opening quotation is from Plato. We are also reminded of Digory's remark in *The Last Battle*: "It's all in Plato, all in Plato . . ." as they enter the other world of full reality. This world and everything in it are mere shadows and images of the perfect and ideal world. So every human story is a shadow, a memory "of the forgotten story in the Magician's Book." It is this Platonism, we feel, that gives such solidity to his description of heaven, where his imagination soars, and we ourselves are caught up in rapture.

"Myth became Fact," where he argues "what flows into you from a myth is not truth but reality." It is a perfect bridge between concrete experience and abstract ideas. This is why he complains in *The Problem of Pain* that a doctrinal explanation of The Fall never does justice to the power of the biblical myth, because only myth releases the actuality of it to the imagination and heart. Elsewhere he talks of myth as "tasted reality," and in the science fiction stories, as well as some of the Narnia stories, he incorporates mythic elements to try to express a heightened sense of reality. For him "the heart of Christianity is a myth which is also a fact. . . . it is perfect myth and perfect fact."

In a sense, then, Lewis saw Christianity as the fulfillment of paganism. Here we begin to see the Romantic nature of his Christian experience. In *The Pilgrim's Regress*, Romanticism is seen as a natural (rather than supernatural) revelation of God, and history is interspersed with such periods of revelation. One such period was that of medieval chivalry, about which he wrote so well in *The Allegory of Love*. A period nearer to hand was the

Loss of Faith

Having established some key concepts in Lewis's thinking and writing, we can now more easily trace the path that led to his conversion. Conversion usually begins with little or no faith. *Surprised by Joy* sets out a loss of "little" faith; *The Pilgrim's Regress* also does so, even if rather less clearly, in its first four books. Lewis's parents were members of the Church of Ireland, but this seems to have made little impact on him. It has been suggested that the Puritania of *The Pilgrim's Regress* must refer to the Protestantism of Ulster; but Lewis denied this, and his autobiography gives no evidence for such an assertion. He rather places his first religious awareness at his first school, where the boys were taken to a High Anglican church, and the fears of hell were laid on them, no doubt reinforced by the school regime, with its arbitrary and merciless punishments.

However, he took his faith seriously enough. But by the time he reached Malvern prep school he was caught in a legalistic struggle to "feel" his prayers. The self-effort required was overwhelming, and he says it was with some relief that he finally dropped Christianity, under the influence of several of the school staff. This led him into several contradictions. The schizophrenia to do with myth we have mentioned. The other was to do with his father's insistence on his being confirmed. He did not dare tell his father of his unbelief, and so "I allowed myself to be prepared . . . and confirmed . . . acting a part." In his escape from the "fear of Christianity," and the "No Admittance" to "the transcendental Interferer" (his phrases) there was perhaps also a reaction to his father's invasion of privacy.

Going to Kirkpatrick was to reinforce unbelief. Later, he described the Great Knock as "a hard satirical atheist who . . . filled his house with the products of the Rationalist Press Association." His letters to Arthur at this time confirm this. Lewis writes: "You know, I think, that I believe in no religion. There is absolutely no proof for any of them . . ." and he develops this theme over several letters. Likewise, the poetry he wrote over the next few years, later published as *Spirits in Bondage*, was similar in its philosophy to Thomas Hardy's: nature is malevolent, and if there be a God, he must be uncaring or incompetent.

The Long Search

Toward the end of his time with Kirkpatrick, Lewis confesses to "intermittent wavering in my materialistic 'faith,'" caused by some of his reading. The Irish poet W. B. Yeats, who described himself as "the last of the Romantics," had constructed his own private, neoplatonic mythology. What struck Lewis was that this respected, non-Christian poet actually believed his mythology and tried to live it out. Later, at Oxford, Lewis took the opportunity to visit Yeats, and was overwhelmed by his charisma. He mentions also the Belgian poet Maeterlinck, who, though again a non-Christian was yet a believer in the spiritual.

George MacDonald

But the biggest single "bombshell" at this time to Lewis's unbelief was the discovery of the Scottish Christian writer, George MacDonald. At first Lewis seems to have played down the impact of reading one of MacDonald's prose fantasies, *Phantastes*, barely mentioning it to Arthur. But later, in his autobiography, and also in an introduction he wrote to another of MacDonald's fantasies, *Lilith*, he talks of the book "baptizing his imagination." It led him into the realms of myth, and yet for the first time he found the quality of "holiness." He had already become aware of the darker sides of Romanticism, but here was "cool morning innocence" and "a certain quality of Death,

George MacDonald.

good Death." He always acknowledged MacDonald to be his main spiritual guide and mentor, and in *The Great Divorce* the figure of MacDonald instructs him in the mysteries of heaven.

We can trace Lewis's reading of MacDonald in his letters to Arthur, as we can his reading during World War I. Without realizing it, Lewis was being attracted to Christian writers. First MacDonald, then G. K. Chesterton, with his "commonsense" approach. Lewis has sometimes been likened to Dr. Johnson in his manner, physical appearance, intellectual capacity, and down-to-earthness and sometimes to Chesterton. Certainly Lewis learned a great deal from both men's ability to express Christian truths directly and concretely.

But it was not just books that influenced Lewis; it was also people. In *The Problem of Pain* he writes "when I first came to Oxford, I was as nearly without a moral conscience as a boy could be. . . . of chastity, truthfulness and self I thought as a baboon thinks of classical

music." He describes the effect of meeting non-Christian soldiers and students who had moral standards and ideals which were clearly not based on material self. His complacency was deeply disturbed.

A "Great War"

Two of these non students, C. Harwood and Owen Barfield, soon became converts to Anthroposophism, a set of beliefs touching somewhat on Christianity. Lewis began a "Great War" with Barfield, by face-to-face argument and by letter, which he describes as one of the turning points in his life. He also found Christian students he liked, one of whom, Nevill Coghill, was in the English school, and became a lifelong friend. In addition he found while reading English that the poets he most liked were all Christian!

On the other hand there were opposing forces, especially the new psychology, which dismissed the spiritual; and several people to whose spirituality he took the strongest dislike. But his "war" with Barfield showed him that just because something was the latest trend did not make it any more likely. The journey to faith was beginning.

The Grand Canyon

In *The Pilgrim's Regress* John finally comes to an enormous chasm right across his road. He has come as far as he can by his own efforts, and those of his companion, Virtue. He meets a figure called Mother Kirk (the Christian gospel) who offers to carry him down one side of this chasm, or "Grand Canyon," and up the other. He refuses, and seeks his own way down by journeying along northward and then southward. Finally, trapped on a narrow ledge, he is confronted by Christ himself, and has to surrender himself to Christ's ways of death to self, and rising to new life through spiritual baptism.

Warren Lewis, Jack Lewis's brother.

The parallel account of his conversion in *Surprised by Joy*, written many years after, has a similar two-stage process, but significantly changes the details. Here the first stage is coming to God, and thus adopting a theistic position. The second stage is realizing who Christ is, and thus embracing Christianity. The stress here is on the first stage, whereas in the *Regress* it is more on the second.

Lewis moved from Idealism, with no idea of a personal God, to Pantheism, the idea of an impersonal God in everything, a stance that a number of Romantics adopted. From there he edged slowly to Theism. He sees it as a natural road, and was surprised at the time that there were so few other seekers. He suggests it may have been because Idealism was no longer in fashion but more likely it was because there are so few seekers—certainly few intellectual seekers—who also have a tremendous desire for spiritual fulfillment.

Most of this took place during the later 1920s, with Lewis secure in his teaching post. He describes some of the temptations of the *dolce vita* of an Oxford don's life in the characters of Mr. Sensible, the cultured hedonist or Epicurean, and Mr. Broad, the liberal, broad-churchman, in *The Pilgrim's Regress*. He was also still seeking to be a poet, working on a long poem, *Dymer*, a sort of medieval fantasy epic. When published it attracted little attention.

Catching and Being Caught

What strikes us in Lewis's accounts of his move toward faith are the metaphors of catching and being caught. He talks of the angler; of chess-playing; of cat and mouse. In human terms, he expresses it in *Voyage to Venus* as the fear of being drawn into something. In theological terms, in *The Problem of Pain*, the language is of "election"; that is, being chosen, even pursued, by God's grace. God is the divine chess-player making the good moves against Lewis, the beginner.

The paradox of "calling" yet "being called" is beautifully portrayed in the Narnia books *The Silver Chair* and *The Horse and his Boy*. Lewis, at one moment, felt he had a perfectly free choice, yet was bound to make only one choice. So ultimately his "search" for truth became God's "search" for him. As he puts it in his autobiography, one might as well talk about the "mouse's search for the cat"! So in the Trinity term of 1929, he writes in the now famous words: "I gave in and admitted that God was God, and knelt and prayed. . . ."

The Pilgrim's Regress

Lewis's final move to Christianity is much less dramatically portrayed in his autobiography. In fact his description of the day he went to Whipsnade Zoo in Warren's motorbike sidecar not a Christian and returned as one seems almost an anti-climax just as is his conclusion about joy: "to tell you the truth the subject has lost nearly all interest for me." For he had come home and found the true source of joy.

In fact, we get perhaps a better picture in his letters to Arthur, which are very frequent and full over the period 1929–31. In them we see the beginnings of a real religious consciousness, with genuine spiritual insights; we see him looking at his moral state (and being horrified at the pride he found in himself); we see him trying to throw off old habits of temper and skepticism. He also writes of his reading of the German mystic Boehme: "I wish to record that it has been the biggest shaking up I've got since I first read Phantastes.... it's a real book, i.e. it's not like a book at all, but like a thunderclap." It gave him new insights into God as creator and of the incarnation. But it was the meaning of redemption that proved the biggest sticking point, and, as we have already seen, Lewis explains to Arthur how his talk on true myth with two Christian friends, Tolkien and Dyson, slotted this into place for him.

Converts usually take strong attitudes and find ways to express these. For Lewis, the immediate way was to write *The Pilgrim's Regress* and to use it, like Bunyan, to demonstrate not only the true way, but also the false pilgrims. On the journey to faith, John discovers their falsity only with difficulty. But John, unlike Christian in *Pilgrim's Progress*, has to make a journey back, when he sees truly; falsities are seen as horrors, not as attractions. On the return also comes the integration of the emotional and intellectual sides of his nature through various ordeals.

Remarkably, he wrote the book in two weeks, giving it to Arthur to comment on. Arthur was not happy about the style of some of the learned references. While Lewis changed a few things, we are still left with a prose work that lacks the qualities of a novel, without quite being a comprehensible

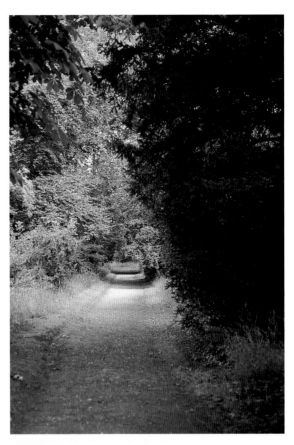

Addison's Walk, Oxford, where Lewis often strolled.

argument for Christianity. Nevertheless, it is overneglected, and shows the way Lewis was to develop as a writer of fiction and as a defender of the rationality and sense of Christianity. He also shows his power to demolish opposition; not just false philosophies, but especially liberal theology. To the very end of his life he abhorred the watering down he saw in liberal theology, and his language stayed as intense as ever. His picture of the modernist bishop returning to hell, in *The Great Divorce*, is not only unforgettable but surprisingly topical. Finally, Lewis discovered his brother had also, in a quiet way, found his own way back to faith, and they were able thus to enjoy a deeper fellowship as Warren came to live at The Kilns.

The Inklings

Right: J. R. R. Tolkien.

Writing to a publisher, Lewis said:

"My happiest hours are often spent with three or four old friends in old clothes tramping together and putting up in small pubs or else sitting up till the small hours in someone's college rooms, talking nonsense, poetry, theology, metaphysics over beer, tea and pipes. There's no sound I like better than adult male laughter."

So who were these "old friends"? We have already mentioned Owen Barfield. Unfortunately, Barfield was not able to stay in Oxford on entering the legal profession, but he kept up his friendship with Lewis, visiting when he could.

Twice Weekly

In 1930 Lewis met Hugo Dyson, a lecturer at Reading University, only a short train journey away. He writes of his first impressions: "He is a man who really loves truth: a philosopher and a religious man . . ." and then describes the curious blend of deadly serious conversation and uproarious laughter that was such a feature of Lewis's style. It was Dyson who was one of the people who helped Lewis to see that myth could be true, and so provided the breakthrough for him to Christianity.

Tolkien

The other friend who helped in this was J. R. R. Tolkien, easily the best known of Lewis's friends at this time. Lewis had first met Tolkien at English faculty meetings and had quite liked him from the start. Tolkien was an Old English specialist who soon achieved professorial status. He was also a committed Roman Catholic. After Lewis's conversion, their friendship blossomed, and, despite Tolkien's being a married man, there were many midnight talks. In 1933 Tolkien showed Lewis the manuscript of *The Hobbit*. Lewis told Arthur: "Reading (it) has been uncanny it is so exactly like what we would both have longed to write (or read) in 1916. . . ." Tolkien also ran a club, the "Kolbitars" (an Old Norse term for those who sit round fires), which was devoted to reading Old Norse myths and legends in the original. Although Lewis had not learned the language, he nevertheless attended keenly.

Another club or society which Lewis attended at this time was called "The Inklings." It had been started by a student for the purpose of members' listening to each others' writings. It was a formal society, with minutes kept, but it dissolved when its founder left Oxford in 1933. However, the name revived informally at some stage over the next few years round a group of friends who met weekly in Lewis's rooms in

The Bodleian library, Oxford.

King's College Chapel, Cambridge.

Magdalen New Buildings, rooms he occupied for thirty years. Their purpose was to read to each other what they had been writing, talk about it, and then discuss more generally any topic that interested them.

Humphrey Carpenter traces the history of this group in his excellent book *The Inklings*. He suggests the group was for encouraging one another, rather than to be a creative writing group as such; but it would be difficult to say what else bound them together. A common disagreement with modernist literature; a commitment to religious truth; a love for mythology have all been suggested. A more human reason would be Lewis's capacity for male friendship and his personal magnetism.

The group was certainly flourishing by 1938, and several attempts have been made to reconstruct a Thursday evening in Lewis's shabby rooms. After a youthful zest for buying well-bound new books, Lewis seems to have gone in for shabby books, or ones from his father's library, actually preferring to use the books in the Bodleian, the main university library. His furniture was equally shabby, as was The Kilns later, after Mrs. Moore became bedridden. Meetings of the Inklings apparently began between nine o'clock and ten-thirty, and would continue till the small hours. It was at such meetings that Tolkien read some of *The Lord of the Rings* and Lewis some of his science fiction and apologetics, though hardly any of the Narnia stories, for the Thursday evenings petered out in the autumn of 1949. Some older members had dropped out by that time, and not all the new ones were so committed or in tune with each other.

"The Bird and Baby"

The Inklings also used to drink beer together on Tuesday mornings at an Oxford pub officially called "The Eagle and Child," but affectionately known as "The Bird and Baby." It stands in St. Giles, and is now somewhat of a mecca for Lewis aficionados. These were informal gatherings for chat and fellowship. Later they moved to another pub called "The Lamb and Flag," and sometimes they went out to a nearby village inn, "The Trout" at

"Ugly as a Chimpanzee"

Two people not mentioned so far in connection with the Inklings are Charles Williams and Lewis's brother, Warren. Although not an academic, Warren keenly enjoyed intellectual discussion and came to act as host for the Inklings. He often worked in Lewis's rooms at college, either assisting Jack or pursuing his own research in French history, which became his particular published interest. We could also mention here some of the better known post-war Inklings: Tolkien's son, Christopher, and J. A. W. Bennett, who later succeeded Lewis as professor at Cambridge. The scholar Lord David Cecil and the writer John Wain also attended at times.

But it was Charles Williams who had the greatest influence on Lewis, who said he owed everything to him and called him his "friend of friends." They seemed to be on exactly the same spiritual wavelength. Writing to Arthur, Lewis described him as "of humble origin (there are still traces of cockney in his voice), ugly as a chimpanzee but so radiant (he emanates more love than any man I have ever known) that as soon as he begins talking . . . he looks like an angel." This electrifying quality of Williams' speaking was witnessed to by many others, including those who heard him lecture at Oxford. Women, it seems, were particularly attracted by these qualities, but clearly Lewis responded equally enthusiastically.

Lewis had first come across Williams in 1936, when reading one of his early novels, *The Place of the Lion*. At that time there was a brief exchange of letters, as Williams was on the editorial staff of the Oxford University Press in London, which was publishing Lewis's *The Allegory of Love*. At the beginning of World War II, the press evacuated back to Oxford, and Williams with it. Immediately he was pressed into the

Inside "The Eagle and Child."

Inklings, where he seemed to fit at once. Lewis described their "Bird and Baby" talk as "so fast and furious that the company thinks we're talking bawdy when in fact we're very likely talking theology."

Although Williams had no formal qualifications, Lewis managed to get him on to the English department lecture program, to teach a course on Milton. The lectures were quite unique, and influenced Lewis in his book *A Preface to Paradise Lost*, which he was writing at the time. But perhaps the greatest literary influence on Lewis was through Williams's fantasy novels where the ordinary world is somehow invaded by outside forces. As Lewis claims in his essay on "The Novels of Charles Williams," illumination is given both on the quality of our everyday lives and also on the spiritual forces of good and evil around us. The change in Lewis's own science fiction, seen in his novel *That Hideous Strength*, can be directly attributed to Williams's fiction. Theologically, too, Williams counteracted Lewis's extreme rationality in his apologetics—Williams showed him that theology contains paradoxes that neither can nor should be resolved logically.

Although Williams was only ten years older than Lewis, he never enjoyed good health. He died quite suddenly in 1945. As a tribute to his friend, Lewis edited the Arthurian epic Williams had been engaged in writing for many years, adding an essay to it; he also contributed to what in effect was the Inklings' homage, *Essays Presented to Charles Williams*, which the Oxford University Press published soon after.

"The Eagle and Child" pub Oxford, favored haunt of the Inklings.

Godstow. This gathering changed to a Monday when Lewis received a Cambridge professorship in 1954, the group usually adjourning to see Lewis off to his train. This continued until his death in 1963, though it was never formally referred to as the Inklings after the Thursday evenings finished.

Recently, efforts have been made to see the Inklings as a highly significant group. The people in it certainly were, and their friendships together were significant to them personally. But to try to see them as "The Christian Romantics" or "Romantic theologians" is to put too formal a categorization on them. Like an earlier Oxford grouping, "The Holy Club," to which the Wesleys belonged, we could perhaps say that people were brought together in committed friendship and fellowship, and out of that was created something far beyond what the group meant or foresaw for itself.

Talks and Apologetics

In a letter to Arthur around the time of his conversion, Lewis wrote:

"From the age of sixteen onwards I had one single ambition, from which I never wavered, in the prosecution of which I spent every ounce I could, on which I really and deliberately staked my whole contentment: and I recognize myself as having unmistakably failed in it."

He was trying to console Arthur at the time and may have exaggerated the sense of his own failure as a poet. It would seem, however, that the sense of failure acted to produce a right sort of humility, for never at any later time does the thought of literary fame touch him, or its actuality. He even used to throw away copies of his own books sent to him by his publishers, as well as many of his original manuscripts.

When World War II began, Lewis's fame was still limited to the academic world, and was largely due to his *Allegory of Love* and his controversy with Professor Tillyard of Cambridge, published as *The Personal Heresy* in 1939. There was nothing to indicate the sudden rise to fame which occurred during the war, and which has continued unabated ever since. The fame needs to be seen coming in two waves: the first, wartime, wave has to do with his defense of orthodox Christianity (technically called "apologetics") against modern unbelief, both secular and theological; the second, in the 1950s, is associated with his children's stories. There is no obvious link between them unless we remember Lewis's twofold nature: the rational, logical philosopher; and the romantic lover of myth and "the horns of elfland." In much of his writing we find one side or the other; in some we have both.

The Problem of Pain

In 1939 Geoffrey Bles, a small publishing company, decided to create "The Christian Challenge" series of books and Lewis was asked to contribute a volume on suffering. Although *The Pilgrim's Regress* had sold few copies, it had gained admirers, and it was through one of these that the invitation came. Lewis had the intellectual stimulus of the Inklings while writing *The Problem of Pain*, as he decided to call the new book. "A little thing," he told Arthur, but it was an immediate success, and continues to be one of his best books.

On first appearance, Lewis struck many people as a "hale and hearty" type of man, very forceful, but perhaps not oversensitive to suffering or weakness. But beneath the appearance there was, in fact, a real vulnerability. He confesses to Arthur many times of great unhappiness, some of which was no doubt occasioned by Mrs. Moore, though he had, of course, also suffered much as a child. The clearest example of his capacity

Painting of the Senior Common Room at Magdalen College. Lewis is on the right.

to suffer came later, in the grief experienced on the death of his wife.

But even if we have established a sympathy in Lewis for his subject matter, his approach to it in the book seems immediately academic and philosophical. The method is typical of him: a ground-clearing operation first, followed by foundation-laying, and only then a building up of the main argument. Readers have to wait some time before they feel they are getting some answers. Lewis holds our attention by giving us confidence that answers will be forthcoming, but the difficulties are real and we need patience. The central theme does not emerge until chapter six: that self-surrender to the will of God is vital, and only when we understand this can we see any purpose in suffering. In this book, some of Lewis's best writing occurs when he

moves away from the strictly logical to paint a picture of man before the fall, or to describe the condition of hell. We feel here that his imagination transforms the logic to present powerful statements, and to set our hearts as well as our minds on God's redemptive purposes, and the hope of heaven.

Lewis's emergence as a champion of orthodox Christianity during World War II is not quite as coincidental as it might appear. Lewis saw his mission as a defender in a spiritual warfare going on in contemporary culture, and that his "war service" was literally to fight for truth. This is what led him, for example, to trek around Royal Air Force camps up and down the United Kingdom giving talks on Christianity to servicemen. But the war also brought a new openness to religion, and Christian publishers found ready markets for their books. Peacetime complacencies were shattered, and the foundations of people's lives were deeply disturbed.

Mere Christianity

It was this new openness that led the B.B.C. (British Broadcasting Corporation) to ask Lewis to broadcast for them, following the success of *The Problem of Pain*. Lewis immediately agreed, though the medium of radio was new to him. The first series was broadcast weekly live in the autumn of 1941. It attracted an immediate response of letters, most of which Lewis felt it his moral duty to reply to. In fact, the first series consisted of two parts: the first seeking to establish that we have an innate sense of law, of right and wrong, and that we need to have a belief in God for that sense to take on any real meaning. The second was to establish the main belief of Christianity: that Jesus was God in man a stupendous claim about which we have to do something.

Bles published the talks the next year, at which time Lewis undertook a second radio series, this time entitled "Christian Behavior." A third series followed in 1944, "Beyond Personality,"which deals with what it is to be a Christian and in relationship with God. The three resulting books were finally combined into one in 1952 as *Mere Christianity*, a phrase taken from the seventeenth-century Christian writer, Richard Baxter, and meaning the basic form and beliefs of Christianity accepted by orthodox believers of all traditions and denominations.

The Screwtape Letters
Also in 1942 probably Lewis's most famous book appeared, *The Screwtape Letters*, having first been serialized in a religious journal. It is the one book Lewis stated he did not enjoy writing, since imagining what one devil might write to another got right inside him and made him feel all "gritty." For all that, the book has immense verve and a weird sort of humor, and again, immediately took hold of the public.

Although Lewis said the idea came to him suddenly in 1940, we can trace origins for it. For example, while at Bookham, he wrote to Arthur Greeves: "I wonder what a book called *Letters from Hell* . . . would be like?" This book, when obtained, was a disappointment, a sort of romantic novel. Another book he read, Stephen McKenna's *Confessions of a Well Woman* (1922), has also been suggested as a genesis. Certainly, the black-and-white polarities of hell and heaven fitted in well with Lewis's style of arguing and imagining, as they did later in *The Great Divorce* (1945), which paints the other side of the picture, the outlook from heaven. These are both much more imaginative, fictional types of work, less obviously intellectual, representing the other strand of his apologetic work: the depiction of certain spiritual states, especially the joys of the heavenly and the miseries of the hellish.

During this period, there existed at Oxford a very lively and flourishing debating society called the Socratic Club, of which Lewis was president. It became a forum for arguments for and against religion, Lewis himself speaking some eleven times in main speeches, as well as consistently taking part in the debate from the floor. In this way, many generations of students were able to hear Lewis at his philosophical, logical best. The only time he seems to have been worsted was in 1947 by a professional philosopher, G. E. M. Anscombe—to make it worse for Lewis, she was a woman and a Catholic—he still had doubts about the intellectual capacities of both categories.

Miracles
Lewis had been writing and talking a lot about the miraculous at this time. To him, Christianity was nothing if not supernatural

and he felt he was up against both materialists and liberal theologians who *a priori* dismissed miracles as "unhistorical" and "unscientific." Thus Lewis's defense was strategic. He endeavors to show that miracles are neither unhistorical nor unscientific, and thus Christianity *is* credible. It has been suggested that after Lewis's "defeat" at the hands of Miss Anscombe, he retired from active apologetics. Certainly, he modified that particular chapter in *Miracles*, but the constant stream of papers and talks that he gave for the rest of his life hardly suggests a defeated man. Lewis was not the sort of person to be put off by one fall in the cut-and-thrust of academic debate.

One last book needs to be mentioned here, *The Abolition of Man* (1943). It starts as an attack on the teaching of English at secondary school level, but it goes on to broaden into a warning about the possible loss of values in our society through skeptical approaches to moral statements of truth, value, and worth, and their reduction to subjective states. Such a warning was indeed prophetic, and that we might feel the confusion of values both in our schools and in our society is exactly what Lewis predicted. The book is not specifically Christian apologetic, appealing to the "Tao" of ancient Eastern wisdom as much as to Greek and Christian concepts.

All this fame, of course, brought Lewis many invitations to speak, preach, and write articles. Much of what he produced for these was of an apologetic nature, sometimes, but not always, on themes covered by the books. A few of these pieces were collected together before his death, for example in *They asked for a Paper*. Two of his best collections of essays are *God in the Dock*, which takes its title from an address on the difficulties of presenting the Christian gospel to modern unbelievers; and *Screwtape Proposes a Toast*, containing two marvelous wartime sermons "The Weight of Glory" and "Transposition," the former preached to a packed Oxford congregation. Not naturally a preacher, these show in Lewis an inspiration worthy of the best.

Other Worlds

Miracles, then, was the last of Lewis's major apologetic works—last not because of any uncertainty about the possibilities of defending Christianity as a rational religion, but because he had said all he wanted to say in that way. He possibly felt also that his arguments were getting too complex and over-academic for the average person in the street, for whom, after all, he was primarily writing. His Royal Air Force talks had convinced him of the vital necessity for simple language.

Science Fiction

Out of the Silent Planet

But for the direction which his writing took in the 1950s, and the second "wave" of fame, we need to look back to 1937, the year Lewis started to write science fiction with *Out of the Silent Planet*. Oxford dons have been known to write such books for light relief, but Lewis's purposes were quite other. Although his first literary ambition had been poetry, he had had a long childhood apprenticeship in prose, writing about an imaginary "Animal Land."

In adolescence he developed an appetite for science fiction, and in his autobiography he suggests that his own science fiction was an exorcism of his "lust" and the "coarseness and eagerness of his original appetite." He was by no means a highbrow reader as he grew older. As his letters to Arthur Greeves show, he delighted in reading and rereading such Victorian favorites as Sir Walter Scott, Wilkie Collins and Rider Haggard. H. G. Wells he much admired, but the book which really showed him the spiritual possibilities of the science fiction genre was David Lindsay's *A Voyage to Arcturus*, a strange allegorical fantasy set on a planet of another universe.

Lewis's own science fiction certainly explores the spiritual possibilities of the form, more or less disregarding the science, though not from ignorance. Lewis was able to discuss scientific ideas intelligently, even without formal training, and indirectly he attacks ideas of such contemporary scientists as Professor J. B. S. Haldane, especially as they are expressed by one of his characters, Weston.

In *Out of the Silent Planet*, the discussion of such ideas starts very cautiously, however. The hero, Ransom, is kidnapped by Weston

C. S. Lewis photographed on
one of his walking holidays.

and his associate, Devine, and finally reaches Malacandra (Mars) where he is to be offered up as some sort of "ransom" so that Weston and Devine can exploit the planet's gold. Ransom himself fears the worst, having imbibed the hitherto current science fiction philosophy that humans are better than aliens, and is amazed to discover that the strange inhabitants of the planet are unfallen beings, who mean good to him, and are ruled over by "Oyarsa," or angelic beings, who serve "Maleldil," or God. Ransom finally has his eyes opened to the fact that only Earth has fallen, ruled over by an evil Oyarsa (Satan), and is thus silent, unable to communicate with the rest of the spiritual universe. Weston and Devine receive no such enlightenment. The plot unfolds logically and simply; the idea is surprising, though the characterization and dialogue are somewhat wooden—difficulties Lewis had in *The Pilgrim's Regress*, his only previous prose fiction work.

Voyage to Venus

The next science fiction is very much more successful all around, and remained Lewis's favorite: *Perelandra* (1943), later reprinted as *Voyage to Venus*. Lewis was also writing on Milton's *Paradise Lost* at the time, and listening to Charles Williams's lectures. He had the Inklings to read the novel to, so it is not surprising that its ideas are far more developed, and that both characterization and plot are more complex. Again, Ransom features centrally, and Weston is the villain— this time meeting a gruesome death as he is taken over by evil forces, becoming the "Unman."

Someone has called the novel "Paradise Retained," for the parallels with Milton's epic are close. Venus is the new Eden, with an unfallen Eve. As with Milton, the woman is separated from her man and is tempted, but this time resists the temptation. Paradise is thus assured for her and her descendants.

As we saw with *The Problem of Pain*, Lewis is very good at imagining humanity before the Fall—much better than Milton. He also avoids Milton's difficulty of making the devil perhaps too attractive, by putting the temptation into the mouth of the Unman—an obviously gruesome being. The temptations are basically the same as Milton's, which are ultimately those of the Genesis account: pride, questioning God's decree, rebellion against hierarchy, and vanity. The temptation scenes are very long and we get a real sense of touch-and-go with them. Like Ransom, we look on, almost helplessly, forgetting, as he does, God's grace given to us all at such moments. The novel ends in a rapture of Platonic idealism, where Greek myth and Christian truth merge in a hymn of joy.

That Hideous Strength

The last fiction, *That Hideous Strength* (1945), is very different, and owes a lot to Williams's influence. It is set, as with Williams's novels, in England in the not-too-distant future. Under the guise of technological advance led by Devine, satanic forces infiltrate the universities and the state apparatus. The spiritual forces of good center around a much wiser Ransom, but the myth of Merlin returned to life is also brought in. Confusion is finally brought on the evil forces, and they are swallowed up in an earthquake.

All this sounds rather unlikely, and the novel does lack a certain credibility all the way through. Merlin and the animals appear particularly ridiculous. Yet for all its very obvious faults, it is by far the most ambitious of the novels and, if anything, fails through trying to say too much. The most successful element is the tracing of the progress of the "modern" young couple, Mark and Jane Studdock, as they learn the realities of spiritual warfare and the need to make black and white choices. By telling the story through their perceptions, Lewis is able to open up to us the nature of human fallenness and the possibilities of grace.

Till We Have Faces

The 1950s were prolific years for Lewis. While completing the Narnia stories between 1949 and 1953, he had fashioned his autobiography, *Surprised by Joy*, which came out in 1955. In that year he was writing what was to become his last and favorite fiction, *Till We Have Faces*, published by Geoffrey Bles the next year, and dedicated to Joy Davidman. If any of Lewis's fiction could be interpreted allegorically, this story would seem to be the one. It is based on the Greek myth of Eros (meaning love; he is the son of Venus), and Psyche (in Greek the word for soul). The story does not occur in the main body of Greek mythology, but only in a book called *The Golden Ass* by a later Roman writer, Apuleius. Psyche's beauty incurs Venus's jealousy and Eros's love. He becomes Psyche's divine lover, but she, instigated by her two jealous sisters, betrays him. To win back his love, Psyche has to perform three seemingly impossible tasks. She does, and is finally immortalized.

Clearly the story has possibilities for Platonic allegory: the soul's search for divine truth, having had an initial fleeting revelation of it. As such, it had haunted Lewis since he was a young man, but he could find no form in which to retell it: he had tried a long poem and failed. At some stage the inspiration came to him to tell the story through the elder of Psyche's sisters, whom he named Orual, using a realistic speaking-voice style. Orual's jealousy is transformed into possessive love, with all its manipulativeness and self-pity. *The Great Divorce* had earlier explored some examples of such possessiveness in action. The plot of *Till We Have Faces* revolves around Orual's complaint against the gods for taking Psyche from her, and her enlightenment as she realizes that "her righteousness is as filthy rags," to use a biblical phrase, that she has no real grounds for her complaint, which is shown to be based on her selfishness.

Lewis called his story "a myth retold," and warned against an allegorical interpretation in a letter: "Much that you take as allegory was intended solely as realistic detail," he writes. Allegory demands a detailed one-to-one interpretation, with a fairly flat characterization, although as was discussed with the *Chronicles of Narnia*, allegory can take on its own complexity. Certainly the story Lewis tells is complex, with multi-layered interpretation, which may take several readings to elucidate, and has the fullest and most rounded characterization by far of any of his stories.

Not all readers may find Lewis's use of the female voice entirely convincing, but in defense it must be said he portrays Orual as a woman who tries to be as much like a man as possible, and to deny her femininity, specifically by wearing a mask to hide her supposed ugliness.

It has been suggested that Orual's character was based on Joy Davidman, who by this time was living near the Lewis brothers. But it could just as much be autobiographical, fictionally incorporating the search for faith that Lewis had been writing about a year earlier in *Surprised by Joy*. It has also been suggested that Orual's veiling and unveiling have to do with Lewis's acknowledging part of his inner feelings suppressed for many years, now being released by the touch of sexual love: his feminine side, it might be said. Or perhaps a better way to put this would be to say that in this story he most fully integrates the two sides of his character: the intellectual side and the romantic side of myth and passion.

Certainly both sides wrestle in Orual's character. Mythic sources, not only Greek, and Christian symbol are also beautifully brought together. The title itself is an integration of Greek phrases to do with self-knowledge and ecstasy and St. Paul's symbolism in 2 Corinthians 3:12–18, of both spiritual sight and transformation. The strength of the book lies, then, in both the complexity of its symbolic patterns and the strength of its human portrayals of beauty, self-pity, and love.

The Four Loves

The theme of human love was continued in *The Four Loves*, which was first broadcast, amid some controversy, in the United States in 1958, and then published in 1960. For many, the categorization of love into friendship, affection, sexual love (*eros*), and divine love (*agape*) has proved to be very helpful. It is the genius of Lewis's writing to categorize and differentiate. It is also its danger: readers can allow themselves to be boxed in by such categories—something that Lewis never allows himself to be, it might be said. Some of the material in the book goes back to *The Great Divorce* and earlier, but Joy's presence must have focused Lewis's mind on the topic sharply, for by now he had married her.

Between the two books just discussed came *Reflections on the Psalms* in 1958, although Lewis had been meditating on the themes in the Psalms for some ten years. One of the most effective parts of this book is Lewis's facing up to the very difficult "angry" Psalms, where curses are poured out on enemies.

Another Joy

UNTIL HIS MID-FIFTIES, THE SHAPE of Lewis's life had been predictable, even given his conversion. An academic, ensconced in a safe career, with a growing reputation both as scholar and writer, he was finally rewarded in 1954 by being offered a newly-created professorial post at the university of Cambridge, the chair of medieval and renaissance literature. Mrs. Moore had died, making domestic life much easier. The only problem was Warren's growing alcoholism, which was spasmodic rather than constant, but enough to cause Jack to say to Arthur: "I embark on the 'holiday' with W. full of the gloomiest forebodings. Let me have your prayers: I am tired, scared and bewildered." For all his drinking bouts, Warren nevertheless produced a number of books and outlived Lewis by ten years.

Shadowlands

It was not this domestic problem that rocked Lewis's even-keeled boat. In surprising and unpredictable ways, it was a new joy that forced itself—or rather herself—into Lewis's life, even against his will, bringing him to new heights and new depths of emotion. At the time, few people knew about Lewis's marriage, and, even after Joy's death and his, close friends did not say much. It was only later, through the TV dramatization and film *Shadowlands* that the relationship came to general public attention, though the facts were already known to Lewis's admirers through the biography by Roger Lancelyn Green and Walter Hooper, and Humphrey Carpenter's book on the Inklings.

As Lewis had become well known for his Christian writings, many people wrote to him or came to him for help. As we have said, he felt it his moral duty to reply to all but the cranks. We know from the collection of letters published under the title *Letters to an American Lady* what a chore this must have been for him at times, yet each letter is courteously and helpfully written. Sheldon Vanauken's *A Severe Mercy* tells dramatically how Lewis's writings and later his friendship brought a brilliant young American couple to faith and then nurtured them in their new-found life in Christ. Poignantly, Sheldon's young wife died at much the same time as Joy did, and there was also a grieving together.

Joy Davidman
Another American who corresponded with Lewis on her way to faith was just this Joy. Born Joy Davidman, of Jewish parents from Eastern Europe who had settled in New York, she early became an atheist, then a communist. She married a fellow communist, William Gresham, and both took up writing careers. They gradually became disillusioned

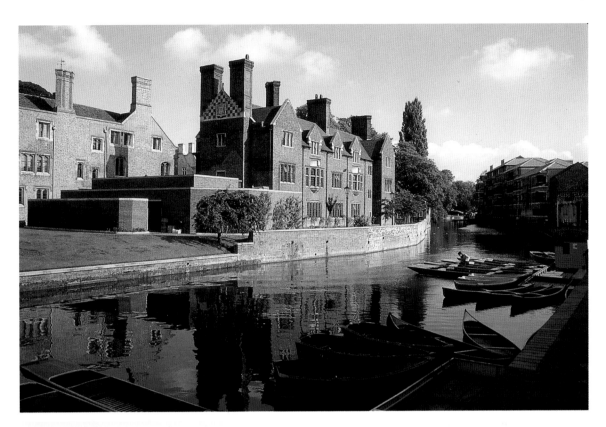

Magdalene College, Cambridge.

with communism, and William suffered a mental breakdown. In her helplessness during this time, Joy had a tremendous experience of God's presence. "I must have been the world's most astonished atheist," she said later. She read *The Screwtape Letters* and *The Great Divorce* and first corresponded with Lewis at that time (1950). The next year both she and her husband became Christians.

Joy talked of all her previous life as "by comparison mere shadow play." We are reminded of Lewis's phrase "the shadowlands" in *The Last Battle*, where the children leave Narnia behind them at death, such was the new reality they had come into. Unfortunately, the new reality could not bind Joy and William Gresham together in what had become a problematic marriage, with two small boys, David and Douglas. Joy felt a period of separation might help, so in 1952 she came to England, inviting Lewis to join her for lunch at an Oxford hotel. He was 54, she was 37.

Two Marriages

The first meeting went well, and was followed by an invitation to The Kilns for Christmas and the New Year. Joy returned to the United States in January 1953, but it became increasingly obvious that her marriage was finished, and later that year she returned to England with the two boys, putting them in school there. Over the winter holidays all three stayed at The Kilns, and Lewis dedicated *The Horse and his Boy*, just ready for publication, to the two boys.

Lewis was in the process of vacating his rooms at Magdalen College, to take up residence at its namesake, Magdalene College, Cambridge; and Joy assisted in this. At first, Lewis wondered whether he had done the right thing in transferring to Cambridge, but he soon settled in, finding the atmosphere of a much smaller college and town congenial, his colleagues much more friendly and

The Kilns, Oxford.

sympathetic, and the teaching load very much lighter. He was allowed to travel to Cambridge on Mondays and return to Oxford on Fridays, and so able to continue living at The Kilns.

In 1955 Joy published an apologetic book of her own, *Smoke on the Mountain*, about the Ten Commandments—her own Jewish background being of great help. Lewis wrote the foreword to it. Even so, finances were getting tight for Joy. Lewis had been helping with school fees, and now he suggested she move to Oxford from London, planning to help pay her rent. She took a house in Headington, and saw Lewis most days. It was quite clear to Warren by this time that she had "designs" on Lewis—she must have fallen in love with him some time earlier. It is unclear exactly what Lewis's feelings for her were at this time. He certainly admired her for her quality of mind and quickness of wit. But he was very reluctant to talk about her, even to Arthur Greeves—he first mentions her

casually only in March 1954, in connection with a testimony she had written for a collection of essays.

Then at the beginning of 1956 came the most extraordinary event, when the British Home Office refused to extend Joy's residence permit. The only way Lewis could see to enable her to stay was to marry her! He called it "a pure matter of friendship and expediency," had the ceremony in a registry office and told no one. Clearly at this stage for him it was not a marriage at all, but a formality. Yet Lewis felt he could not keep visiting her at her house without bringing some scandal on her. Yet how could she live at The Kilns except as his real wife? So he went as far as publishing a notice of the marriage.

Cancer

Then suddenly what Joy had thought of as rheumatism was diagnosed as bone cancer. She was hospitalized and bore the suffering bravely. Whether or not Lewis was in love

Right: Anthony Hopkins and Debra Winger in a still from the film *Shadowlands.*

with her before, certainly he was now. He determined on a "proper" marriage with a clergyman. But Joy, having been divorced, was not eligible for the rites of the Church of England. Nevertheless, God supplied an Anglican clergyman, a former student of Lewis's, from outside the diocese. The clergyman also had a gift of healing, and, at the service, offered to anoint Joy.

Slowly, healing took place. Lewis refused to hope too much. But by the end of the year, Joy was walking slowly, and the following year was able to leave hospital. His own health had not been good at this time—high blood-pressure and osteoporosis—and with Warren's alcoholism, there were times when Jack Lewis felt very low indeed. He tells Arthur: "At any rate, when life gets very bad . . . a sort of anesthesia sets in. There is a mercy in being always tired." Yet three months later he writes: "Our news is all very good. Joy's improvement has gone beyond anything we dared to hope. . . . my osteoporosis is also very much better . . . (although) I don't think I'll ever be able to take a real walk again."

The next two years, 1958 and 1959, were happy. Warren wrote: "What Jack's marriage meant to me was that our home was enriched and enlivened by the presence of a witty, broadminded, well-read tolerant Christian whom I had rarely heard equaled as a conversationalist . . ." though elsewhere Warren clearly misses his close one-to-one relationship with Jack.

"The Sword of Damocles," as Lewis described it, fell in October 1959; cancer spots were returning. Nevertheless the trip to Greece that Joy had set her heart on went ahead, by plane, car, and wheelchair. Lewis had not been abroad since his soldier days but went willingly, together with the Lancelyn Greens. It was wonderfully happy, according to Green's account in his biography. On their return, Joy had a mastectomy, which stayed the cancer for a short while, but it finally overtook her, and she died on 13 July 1960.

A Grief Observed

Joy died saying to the chaplain, "I am at peace with God." Lewis's grief at her death was anything but peaceful. For a while he remained stunned, and then, as a way to express it, he began writing down his thoughts and feelings in four old exercise books he found in the house. When he had finished he sent them to a different publisher from his usual one, under the name of A. Clerk. They were published in 1961 with the title *A Grief Observed*. He never talked about this book, nor gave copies to any friends. Only after several years was it republished with his own name on it.

The book parallels *Till we have Faces*, in that it is a Job-like complaint against God for taking Joy from him. God remains silent, as do the gods when Orual vents her anger, rage, and self-pity at them. But finally, the very silence of God became the answer, for in it is revealed deeper truths about himself. Although much of it is self-centered, there is yet an impassioned desire to know the truth of the matter: is God really good in the way we understand good; or is there the possibility, as he first raises in *The Great Divorce*, of good not being good at all?

Lewis's Grief

Lewis's grief, then, found fullest expression in a literary form and showed itself as a passionate doubting. The calm arguments of *The Problem of Pain* or even *The Four Loves* lie unheeded. For instance he wrote in *The Four Loves*: "Love anything and your heart will certainly be wrung and possibly broken" and "We shall draw nearer to God, not by trying to avoid the suffering inherent in all loves, but by accepting them and offering them to him; throwing away all defensive armor." Such consolations seemed to be deliberately refused. Why should this have been so?

First we must realize that Lewis had been

Joy Davidman.

married only a few years. From what he writes here, his love was as intense as a younger man's, and a great deal more satisfying. He writes: "What was H. [Joy] not to me? She was my daughter and my mother, my pupil and my teacher, my subject and my sovereign; and always, holding all these in solution, my trusty comrade, friend, shipmate, fellow-soldier. My mistress . . ." Thus the emotional intensity of first love was still with him, as well as the sense of loss of a precious gift given to him later in life when all hope of such a gift had gone.

Secondly, we need to see that Lewis was really a very black-and-white person, not just in the dialectic manner of his apologetics, but temperamentally. God is either all loving or all evil; Lewis's loss seems at first entirely evil. He was also a very passionate man; the academic life had disguised this as well as his boyhood fear of emotion. His biographers comment: "[the marriage was] the overwhelming fulfillment of an intense nature long unsatisfied, a tremendous capacity for love long channeled into strong friendship and immense literary creativeness." Lastly, we may presume that grief for his mother's death, so long ago suppressed, was reawakened: he mentions his mother's death of cancer several times in his complaint, and something of the "grief overwhelmed in horror" about her death mentioned in his autobiography emerges now. So the terrified child grieves alongside the adult in Lewis.

An Evil Spell?

Even though this may help explain the intensity of grief, we still need to ask why Lewis chose to publish such expressions. Chad Walsh, in his *The Literary Legacy of C. S. Lewis*, suggests that the book is something of an evil spell—but was publication needed to exorcise it? Is not such public grief merely embarrassing, and complaining against God undermining of what he had previously written?

We need here to see Lewis as a public person: it is one of the characteristics of a true artist that everything is displayed. Possibly Lewis had no thoughts of publication when he started to write, but by the third section he is clearly writing to communicate with others, not just with God or himself. We can perhaps also discern deeper purposes here: to show us that most great Christians have very real crises of faith and agony of spirit. They are not plaster saints, who make merely rhetorical gestures toward suffering. And for the sake of others who suffer such grief, they need to know this is the shape grief can take.

Did Lewis actually lose his faith? The book can be read either way, but the most natural reading is to see his faith being tested rather than destroyed. To Lewis at the time there seemed to be a destroying, but even he finally realized "my idea of God . . . has to be shattered time after time." Breakthroughs do come: he finally senses Joy's presence rather than her absence; he finally experiences bereavement as part of love. And certainly in what he wrote in the remaining few years of his own life, there is no hint of loss of faith, though "The Seeing Eye" (1963) does dwell a great deal on façades. But his faith was not a sham, as he feared in his grief. Would Joy, whom he praised for seeing through all his sham, not have seen through that too?

C. S. Lewis:
Teacher and Critic

We now cover briefly the last few years of Lewis's life. To do this, we need to return to his move to Cambridge. Just before his appointment there he had completed his mammoth volume in the Oxford History of English Literature series (which he called "O Hel," such a chore did it finally become). Chapter one contains a brilliant tracing of patterns of thought and literature in the sixteenth century, and then proceeds to look in more detail at certain individual writers.

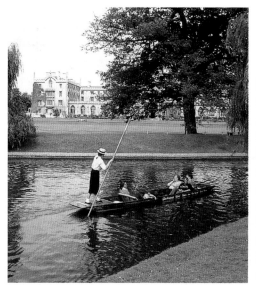

Punting on the backs, Cambridge.

the Elizabethan to the medieval. After his death, Alistair Fowler put together others of his lectures in *Spenser's images of life* (1967). He also received many academic honors, in the form of honorary doctorates, though the first honor he was ever offered (a C.B.E. in 1951) he had refused.

It is the custom of newly installed professors to give inaugural addresses. Lewis's lecture at Cambridge was given the grand title of *"De Descriptione Temporum"* (On describing the times), and the humorous alternative "The Last of the Dinosaurs." In it he deals mainly with matters of literary and cultural history. He concludes that since the beginning of the nineteenth century we have lived in an age different from any that has existed before— "The Machine Age." It is increasingly cut off from the culture of the past, including the values and beliefs of Christianity. He sees this as a decline into a new Dark Ages, and he sees himself as one of the few people still in contact with the life and traditions of our previous Western Christian culture.

The Last of the Dinosaurs

Lewis did not produce any further academic writing until 1960, when his *Studies in Words* came out, followed the next year by *An Experiment in Criticism*, an interesting, if not wholly successful, attempt to set up a new approach to literary criticism and theory. Lastly, some of his Cambridge lectures were incorporated into *The Discarded Image* (1963), which could be seen as a parallel to *The Allegory of Love*, but working backward from

This is a difficult stance to come to terms with. Certainly we are in crisis times, as both *Out of the Silent Planet* and *That Hideous*

Headington parish church, Oxford.

Gravestone of C. S. Lewis.

Strength seek to show. But does Lewis rather enjoy the stance of the embattled minority, as Owen Barfield and J. A. W. Bennett suggest in *Light on C. S. Lewis*? Again, in *The Last Battle*, the feeling of the remnant is very strong. It could be argued this is entirely biblical, and we must stand unflinching in the face of heresy and the spirit of the age. But it does tie Christianity very closely to a declining culture, and suggest an undue pessimism for the future of the faith.

Letters to Malcolm

Lewis was engaged at this time on one last devotional/apologetic book, completed just before his death: *Letters to Malcolm: chiefly on prayer*, begun in 1962. He had been contemplating a book on prayer for some time, but was not able to find the right form for it. Suddenly the idea of a series of imaginary letters came to him perhaps modeled on his long correspondence with Arthur. It is no model guide on how to pray, but a probing debate into what it means to pray, to be a praying creature. The style is conversational and it is difficult to realize that there isn't a real Malcolm at the other end, since his replies are so well imagined.

In the summer of 1961 Lewis needed an operation on his prostate gland, but because of a weakness in his heart and kidneys this was not possible. His health was very seriously undermined, partly by the hard work he had subjected himself to; partly perhaps by a diet that was, by modern standards, unwise; and partly by the growing inability to exercise in the vigorous and healthy way he had earlier. In the summer of 1963 he almost died, attended by only a few friends. He recovered, somewhat reluctantly, but resigned his Cambridge post. Warren returned from a holiday in Ireland and the two brothers spent two months together, waiting, as Warren said, for the new term to begin. On 22 November 1963 Lewis slipped away quietly. He had often anticipated an entry into heaven—at the end of *The Screwtape Letters* and *The Last Battle*. Now he had come home.

Teacher and Critic

Lewis's teaching career spanned forty years, representing some thirteen generations of students. Lewis's personal students included the critic Kenneth Tynan, the novelist John Wain, the writer Roger Lancelyn Green, the poet Sir John Betjeman and Professor John Lawlor. The Oxford system consists of a voluntary lecture series with compulsory weekly tutorials where each student reads out his or her assignment, which is then discussed. Many lecturers find their lectures poorly attended, therefore. Lewis never had this problem: twice a week for six weeks, forty minutes each lecture, his series were popular and inspirational, as well as being scholarly and pitched at the right level. As we read them in such books as *The Discarded Image*, we

C. S. Lewis at his writing desk.

The "gleaming spires" of Oxford.

sense two things: first, a clarity of mind, which is able to find significant patterns in the historic flow of literary texts; secondly, a real desire to communicate to an interested, but not necessarily knowledgeable, audience. Thus he is courteous, and willing to explain at some length, rather than dazzle with exhibitions of learning or technical jargon.

We can perhaps be a little more specific here in terms of his style. His material is very accessible: we can read an essay on a poem without having read the poem, and yet follow it, enjoy it, and even want to read the original. He is able to convey a taste of it, quickly giving us a perception of the key concepts and its relationship with better works. We are treated as human beings, not as disembodied minds. Many of his examples are taken from everyday experience, and we feel our common humanity with him.

Lewis is best at commending literature; less certain in criticizing it. He tries to anticipate our difficulties in reading and divert possible prejudices. Mostly this works very well, but sometimes we are put off by having imaginary objections that we have never actually thought of loaded on to us.

As a tutor Lewis was not quite so successful. He had learned his face-to-face methods from the Great Knock—challenging statements and "picking an argument." Unfortunately, most students did not enjoy such a dialectic method and were quickly reduced to confusion. He treated most of them as if they had first-class minds, already quite able to argue. It is perhaps no wonder he found tutorials rather a chore, and was relieved when, on becoming a professor, he could dispense with them.

There were perhaps other limitations. Lewis's dialectic method of arguing tends to rely on an either/or pattern of thought that sometimes reduces things too quickly to black and white. Whilst this is often a tremendous strength in philosophy or apologetics, it does not always work quite so well in dealing with literature.

A second limitation, as a teacher of English, was that most of the creative and influential thinking on the subject during the mid-twentieth century was going on at Cambridge under such scholars as I. A. Richards, William Empson, F. R. Leavis, and E. M. W. Tillyard. Oxford had locked itself into a languageversus-literature struggle which ultimately proved peripheral to the mainstream of English studies.

Thus, while Lewis's academic contributions to his chosen field of medieval and sixteenth-century literature were much admired, and remain required reading for students, his more general critical and theoretical thinking was not. It is not so much that it was unfashionable, but that its expression primarily in terms of Greek philosophy, either Platonic or Aristotelian, become traditional restatements of positions, ultimately adding little to a Christian philosophy of literature or engaging current thinking.

An Experiment in Criticism, written after his move to Cambridge, is his boldest effort, but it only sketches out a line of thought, and in fact raises as many questions as it answers. Lastly, being a "lover of the past,"Lewis was perhaps unduly hostile to modern literature. He shared with Barfield the belief that language was in decline; and saw the break of traditional literary forms as part of that decline.

What we have positively, though, far outweighs such limitations. We have a brilliant communicator, able to awaken a love for literature in his audience. We have a scholar with a depth of learning extending not only over his chosen field, but over several others—philosophy, classical literature, theology—with an ability to cross-reference and combine into striking generalizations— perhaps the most striking being his argument in the Oxford History that the term "renaissance" as applied to English literary history has little, if any, meaning. His tracing of continuities represents a mind able to see original patterns amidst a mass of detailed work. As Professor Bennett said of him: "He was a Johnsonian colossus rather than a dinosaur."

The Fighter

We have already discussed most of Lewis's major books of Christian apologetics. In one sense, of course, all of Lewis's work is to some extent apologetic, for it is seeking both to defend the Christian gospel and commend it. But it is mainly from those books which come into the stricter category of apologetics that we should draw conclusions about his qualities as an apologist. There are so many points to be made that it is hard to know where to begin. The order chosen here has no special logic to it.

Firstly, we must note that Lewis always writes as a layman to laymen. He said once, at an "Any Questions" session held in a factory: "I am only a layman, and I don't know very much." He always stated he was willing to be corrected by those who knew better, that is, professional theologians. In fact, this was a little disingenuous; he clearly knew a lot, and he clearly became increasingly distrustful of professional theologians, at the end of his life calling some of them prostitutes. But he never forgot he was talking to an "ordinary audience." In an interesting talk he once gave to Anglican clergy on "Christian Apologetics" he even suggested that they should sit an exam in translating religious talk into everyday speech before being allowed into the pulpit.

For all that, his style is carefully chosen. He makes great use of analogies and images to convey his points—not just as useful examples, but because he realized that imagery speaks powerfully to the imagination, which then predisposes the intellect to hear what is being stated. His style is, as Chad Walsh states, flexible, gracious, and clear. It needs to be "modest," that is, low-key enough to allow the ideas to come through; "transparent," yet strong enough to bear the weight of often very difficult concepts. Lewis's grounding in logical thought and good literary style come together perfectly for this task.

Supremely Confident

Lewis is a supremely confident writer: he has confidence in the rational method, in the truth of his convictions, and in the reality of his own journey to Christ—or to put it another way, of his own calling by Christ. Nevertheless, as has been pointed out, he always chose his own ground; he knew his own strengths. Yet he was not necessarily a "safe" thinker, merely repeating in a more elegant or clever way what many had said before. He was prepared to speculate and let his imagination soar, for example in the realities of heaven and hell, into the beauty of Eden or the nature of animal pain. And it has been said rightly that Lewis, in seeking to restate traditional truths, in fact succeeds in being highly original, such is his ability to translate tradition into modern language and images.

Lewis saw clearly that these traditional truths must be the agreed basics for all Christians. Thus he was at the same time non-denominational, convinced of the basic unity of all Christians and Christian attitudes, values, and thought; yet he is also against all modern theology which waters down or demythologizes these truths. But he will not fit easily into an evangelical or liberal categorization. The most that can be said is that it is perhaps in the Church of England that such a non-partisan stance can most easily be maintained, and that if there is any "church" coloring to his writing, it is a middle-of-the-road Anglicanism. But this has never been a barrier. His grief is at the division of Christianity, and the movement of his writing is always towards unity.

Lastly, Lewis is a fighter: sometimes his stance is that of the embattled minority; sometimes of the debater who can pick off his opponents' arguments with consummate ease. The fight is out of an uncompromising desire for truth, however unpleasant. He has no time for "decency" or "kindness" if they become substitutes for truth, since such decency would finally become evil. Only truth has the strength to resist evil.

Defense and Attack

A fighter needs to know both how to defend and how to attack: indeed it is often stated that the best form of defense is attack. Lewis

knew this instinctively—he had a sure sense of when to attack. His timing is perfect. And, to make things more difficult, he had to wage two fights at the same time. The first was against complete unbelief. His defense was that Christianity does make sense: it is not outdated, unscientific, or unhistorical. His attack was that it is the only thing that makes sense. So he attacks the spirit of the times as "temporal provincialism" the contradiction of our age that says truth is all relative, and yet our relativism is absolutely right.

As early as *The Pilgrim's Regress* we get some brilliant knock-down arguments against competing philosophies; even if Christianity is difficult to make sense of, at least it is not full of the contradictions that other belief systems contain. *The Abolition of Man* is another such frontal attack, not so much on explicit philosophies of the age, but on the unstated half-truths of the twentieth century's reductionism: everything can be explained away in terms of something else, and there is no ultimate truth of any value.

The second fight is against forms of theological unbelief. Thus Lewis's defense is that only orthodox Christianity, miracles and all, makes sense. The attack is against liberal Christianity, which he sees as reductionist, busily cutting away the branch on which it is sitting in an attempt to make it palatable to modern people. He exposes its contradictions. He is not one of those "that know [but] have grown afraid to speak," to quote *The Great Divorce*.

Teacher and Expositor

But he is not just a fighter; he is a superb teacher and expositor, setting out, in books such as *Mere Christianity*, just what Christians believe, and how to understand Christianity's truths and mysteries correctly. He never underestimates the difficulties of believing, and in so much of his teaching we also see the

Right: A late photographic portrait of C. S. Lewis.

imaginative artist, able to convey to us just what it feels like to be a Christian, and what certain spiritual states are like. Here we see his early search for joy fulfilled—both transcendent and yet at the same time earthly. Lewis has the artist's ability to clothe the spiritual in the physical, at the same time forming a unity, a oneness of being.

There were limitations, of course. Sometimes we feel there is an overconfidence in the rational, though some of the later books, such as *The Four Loves*, help to correct that. He himself acknowledges freely that the old-fashioned evangelist, with his straight-to-the-heart message, can often accomplish far more than his apologetic methods. This is a due humility. What is a little dangerous at times is his dialectic method of reducing options to just two: either this or that. Sometimes it works brilliantly; at other times it leads to oversimplification. Or it can lead to a rhetorical stance. We get the impression of real arguments, but when we try to use them ourselves, we never find an opponent who quite fits into the argument; or we seem to find the argument dissolves in our hands. One reason for this may be that insufficient biblical perspective is given us; Lewis does not always adequately ground us in biblical foundations.

But these are small things compared with the achievement of making Christians feel confident in their faith, and of challenging non-Christians in their disregard for Christian truth, or their complacent rejection of what is often a Sunday school pastiche of the real thing. Lewis makes us feel the Christian gospel is powerful, to the "breaking down of strongholds," those of the mind and those of the heart.

Critics

In trying to make a balanced assessment of Lewis's achievement, we need to face up to various criticisms that have been leveled against Lewis—at least to the sensible ones, for there are plenty of silly ones, such as that Lewis's literary criticism was sadly wanting because he did not read German! In fact, he did.

We would expect certain groups to attack Lewis, anyway—for instance liberal theologians. After all, they are only fighting back. Or groups who have set up tests into which Lewis will not fit, such as fundamentalists. He cannot be fitted into their beliefs, say, on the inerrancy of Scripture; and, what is worse, his life could be seen as very "worldly" (even though he gave away up to two thirds of his income) since he drank and smoked. We have such criticisms at one extreme; at the other, there is uncritical veneration—whatever Lewis said must be right.

Even at the time of his writing, Lewis's attitude to women was somewhat suspect. With the growth of feminist criticism, this has been highlighted, and Lewis, for most feminists, must by now be outside the pale. In extenuation, we need to remember that he lost his mother early; had no sisters; went to all-boy schools; and attended an all-male college. Early twentieth-century academic life was very male-orientated. The woman he first came close to, Mrs. Moore, he did devote himself to, even though, by his brother's account, she was demanding, silly, and unable to argue logically in any way. If his female personal students found him intimidating, so did most of his male ones. When he did marry, there seems to have been a great equality between himself and Joy, as well as tremendous admiration for her. The marriage seems at the very least to disprove any charge of misogyny.

Right: The film *Shadowlands* retold the story of C. S. Lewis's marriage to Joy Davidman. Anthony Hopkins portrayed Lewis.

Cliques

One of Lewis's earliest preoccupations perhaps derived from his father, and reflected even in his boyhood writing, is with cliques—a problem he found insurmountable at Malvern College. Yet in a sense the Inklings could be seen as a clique, and in *That Hideous Strength*, the clique mentality almost makes the forces of good look absurd. There is clearly a thin dividing between the "remnant" idea, which is thoroughly biblical, and an "Elijah complex," where you need to be reminded that there are "seven thousand who have not bowed the knee to Baal." Perhaps again in extenuation we need to remind ourselves that for most of Lewis's life the Christian church in the United Kingdom was on the decline. Yet his "clique" mentality seems to exist apart from his faith—perhaps a little part of his personality that remained unbaptized.

Conservative

Certainly Lewis was conservative by nature. Most lovers of the past are. Politically, however, he was very skeptical and uninterested—too much so for many people, who feel Lewis should have been addressing current issues more directly. Lewis was not undemocratic, however—"free Narnia" is an important theme, as is the basic equality of its inhabitants. His views on hierarchy, which are anathema to certain egalitarians, are completely biblical, and he always defended them as such. There is, in fact, for those who look impartially, a beautiful balance between equality and hierarchy in his writings.

From a conservative theological viewpoint, certain of his views do seem questionable and unscriptural—for example, those on limbo and purgatory. It is noticeable that his views on purgatory get in the way of his finding consolation in *A Grief Observed*—Joy will merely continue her suffering there. And, as Michael Christensen points out in his *C. S. Lewis on Scripture*, Lewis's views on the Bible would probably please neither liberal nor fundamentalist. These views are not obtrusive, however, since his main job was to concentrate on the basic truths of the faith, which are entirely orthodox.

In these days of what might be termed the "occult explosion," Lewis's references to magic and even astrology become problematic, even though harmless when first written. The tendency of fantasy writing for children has today unfortunately veered toward the occult. Lewis cannot be blamed for that, but the attempt to explain Christian mysteries in terms of "deep magic" has to be rejected, since the connotations are now all wrong.

None of these criticisms can really be considered damning when weighed against the very obvious merits of his life and work. In fact, it could be argued that the most serious limitations are actually none of the above, but those mentioned in the last section: an overconfidence, at times, in human reason, and an oversimplification into an either/or dialectic which does not quite reach people where they are. But in everything he did, there was a massive honesty, an integrity, and a grasp of truth which brings great solidity. With someone like this, critical arrows often bounce back on to the archer.

Lewis's Achievement

How does one measure a person's achievement, especially when he has such a multi-faceted life as Lewis? We could start with the measurable—for instance, sales of his books. Usually, after twenty years, most authors' popularity begins to wane—not so Lewis's. In fact, between his death and 1975, sales of his books trebled!

Individual titles have equally impressive records: *The Screwtape Letters* was reprinted eight times before the end of 1942; total sales of its paperback editions now well exceed one million. C. S. Lewis societies have sprung up, especially in the United States where his popularity is greater than in the United Kingdom.

We might prefer to judge Lewis's achievement in terms of human lives changed. We have many such testimonies. Sheldon Vanauken we have already mentioned. He comments on Lewis's gift of friendship, "the most genial of companions." Vanauken read, wrote to, and met Lewis.

Changed Lives

But many have been changed just by reading his books. One of the most remarkable testimonies of this in recent years is that of Charles Colson, imprisoned for his part in the Watergate affair of ex-president Richard Nixon. While in prison he read *Mere Christianity*, and was struck by the intellectual and logical quality of its defense of Christianity, and by its exposure of human pride. He felt the book spoke exactly to his condition, and testifies to its being an important step in his conversion. As a result of this he founded the Prisoners' Christian Fellowship.

So far, we have measured achievement by what Lewis wrote and did. But very often literary figures such as Dr. Johnson have become famous not just by what they did, but also who they were as people. Lewis certainly seemed to have a similar charismatic quality, indelibly impressing people who met him. A former student, Kenneth Tynan, remembered him for his prodigious memory, his debating skill, his ability to make his chosen field of literary study come alive, and his pastoral concern and humanity.

Jocelyn Gibb collected the comments of close friends in *Light on C. S. Lewis* just after Lewis's death. His friend Nevill Coghill's remarks are particularly apt. He, too, makes the parallel with Johnson. On the other hand, Lewis's stepson David Gresham wrote in a letter that he remembers Lewis being clumsy, irascible, and nervous.

Perhaps the most amusing anecdote is that of Lewis's taxidriver Clifford Morris. Sometimes he would drive Lewis to Cambridge, instead of his taking the train. They might stop at transport cafés for Lewis's compulsory cup of tea. Morris remembers Lewis "sitting in the middle of a crowd of lorry-drivers . . . while he enthralled them with his wit and conversational powers." This shows something of the humility of Lewis and his enjoyment of the society of his fellow human beings—his ability to stay in touch with them despite the ivory towers of Oxbridge.

We can perhaps best sum up Lewis's achievement by saying that here is a man who has really made an impact on his world. And his world is not just the academic one; it is that of the university of life as experienced by ordinary men, women, and children. It is, if you like, the "post-Christian" world of modern Western civilization. His achievement here was to take old truth and give it new relevancy and vitality in a secular age, and to challenge the new complacencies of that age. Part of his continuing impact must be that these complacencies are now well and truly shaken, and people are now more open to reconsider beliefs that claim ultimacy and truth.

Lewis must also be seen as one of those people used by God to turn around the spiritual current of an age. Orthodox Christianity was on the retreat at the time of his conversion by both liberal theology and scientific and secular skepticism. At his death, the Christian church in the United Kingdom, and even more so in the United States, was entering renewal, with Christians emerging from their ghetto with new confidence and hope. Lewis's impact must be acknowledged in this.

Traditional but Radical

Lewis was very traditional in his attitude to worship and church structures, he was radical in the completeness of his conversion—it

This road in Headington is now named after C. S. Lewis.

entered practically every part of his life, so that we feel he really engaged with the world as it actually existed. Even his last essay "We have no 'Right to Happiness,'" shows him addressing contemporary problems, not in despairing gestures, but as a logical, reasonable defender of traditional Christian morality, his thought built on a massive foundation of truth, honesty, and experience. It is his massive balance that stays with us, the balance of imaginative faith and radiant hope, in the spirit of love and charity.

Into the Twenty-first Century

The centenary of Lewis's birth in 1998 came, was marked by many conferences, workshops, festivals, and meetings, and went. But his popularity shows no sign of abating as we move into the twenty-first century. The sales of his books have continued to remain as high as ever. There may not yet be a complete works of C. S. Lewis issued, though Lewis's publishers, both British and American, have brought out uniform editions in various collections and arrangements. Lewis's editors, particularly Walter Hooper, continue to issue or reissue his papers, letters, and minor works. In fact, at the time of writing, it could still be said that not everything Lewis ever wrote and which was not destroyed before or at his death has yet reached print, though that time must be drawing near.

But it is not just the publication and sales of Lewis's books that mark his continued influence and popularity. Countless study groups, both secular and religious, meet to discuss his works. And with the coming of the World Wide Web, numerous websites have been developed from 1994 onwards devoted to aspects of Lewis. Many of these contain news of the various C. S. Lewis societies and study centers that have sprung up around the world. Some of these societies also produce newsletters and magazines; others, such as the C. S. Lewis Institute, also run conferences regularly. These societies can perhaps best be classified into those which deal specifically with Lewis's works (and also, sometimes, those of the other Inklings); and those which deal more generally with themes that are typical of Lewis's concerns, usually focusing on the clash of Christianity with contemporary cultural values, mores, and philosophy; the development of scientific thinking; and other spiritual and apologetic issues relating to Lewis's thinking.

Lewis Studies

As might also be expected, many books about Lewis continue to appear, some popular, some scholarly and some biographical. The number of PhD theses in Lewis studies continues to rise. Archive centers, such as the Marion E. Wade Library at Wheaton College, Illinois, are kept busy, and Lewis's old house in Oxford, The Kilns, has been lovingly restored over a period of ten years and now serves as a study center for Lewis scholars. It was opened by the C. S. Lewis Foundation in 2001. It hosts regular seminars and a visiting scholar program, and is also open to visitors on a limited basis. The old lake is now a nature conservancy, though unfortunately some of the grounds have been sold for new housing.

However, it is in the arena of television and cinema that most recent readers will be aware of the growing interest in Lewis. In the late 1980s, British television brought out a version of *The Chronicles of Narnia*, and we have already mentioned a version of the play *Shadowlands*, based on the love affair of Lewis and Joy. The original play ran to packed houses in London's West End and New York's Broadway. At much the same time, a film was also made of the play. Both Joss Ackland and Anthony Hopkins, who play the part of Lewis in the television and film versions respectively,

give very convincing, though different, portrayals of Lewis. Various television documentaries have continued to be made on Lewis's life and thought, for instance the American PBS documentary *The Magic Never Ends*. And with the publication of this book comes the first of the film versions of *The Chronicles of Narnia*.

Inevitably the mass media has spawned its own commercial empire, from Narnia memorabilia and toys to video games. C. S. Lewis is definitely a profitable business, not a development he would have welcomed any more than his fellow Inkling, J. R. R. Tolkien, would have welcomed his own parallel success. Lewis's own practice was to give away all his commercial profit, largely royalties, to charity. It is to be hoped that the C. S. Lewis Company and others continue this practice.

Countless testimonies continue to come forth, not only of the pleasure that Lewis's books give and the scholarly enthusiasms they continue to awaken, but also of the lives impacted by the clarity and sympathy with which the perennial truths of Christianity and the reality of spiritual values have been presented by C. S. Lewis. There seems little to indicate that production or popularity will abate in the near future. In the crosscurrents of contemporary spirituality they may well increase.

Further Reading

Books by C. S. Lewis

With original publishers and dates, and dates of first paperback edition.

Christian Writing

The Problem of Pain (Centenary Press, 1940; Collins Fontana, 1957)

The Screwtape Letters (Geoffrey Bles, 1942; Collins Fontana, 1955)

The Abolition of Man (Oxford University Press, 1943; Macmillan, N.Y., 1965)

Miracles: a preliminary study (Geoffrey Bles, 1947; Collins Fontana, 1960)

Mere Christianity (a revised edition of *Broadcast Talks* (1942), *Christian Behavior* (1943) and *Beyond Personality* (1944))(Geoffrey Bles, 1952; Collins Fontana, 1955)

Surprised by Joy: The shape of my early life (Geoffrey Bles, 1955; Collins Fontana, 1959)

Reflections on the Psalms (Geoffrey Bles, 1958; Collins Fontana, 1961)

The Four Loves (Geoffrey Bles, 1958; Collins Fontana, 1963)

A Grief Observed (Faber and Faber, 1961; 1966)

Letters to Malcolm: chiefly on Prayer (Geoffrey Bles, 1964; Collins Fontana, 1966)

Literary Criticism

The Allegory of Love: A study in medieval tradition (Clarendon Press, 1936)

The Personal Heresy: a Controversy (Oxford University Press, 1939)

A Preface to Paradise Lost (Oxford University Press, 1942)

Arthurian Torso (on Charles Williams)(Oxford University Press, 1948)

English Literature in the Sixteenth Century (OHEL Vol. III) (Clarendon Press, 1954; re-issued as *Poetry and Prose of the Sixteenth Century*, OHEL Vol. IV, 1990)

Studies in Words (Cambridge University Press, 1960)

An Experiment in Criticism (Cambridge University Press, 1961)

The Discarded Image: an introduction to Medieval and Renaissance literature (Cambridge University Press, 1964)

On Stories: and Other Essays on Literature ed. Walter Hooper (Harcourt Brace, 1966)

Spenser's Images of Life ed. Alistair Fowler (Cambridge University Press, 1967)

Selected Literary Essays ed. Walter Hooper (Cambridge University Press, 1969)

Fiction

The Pilgrim's Regress: An allegorical apology for Christianity, reason and romanticism (Dent, 1933; Eerdmans; Collins Fount, 1958)

Out of the Silent Planet (John Lane, 1938; Pan, 1952)

Perelandra (John Lane, 1943)=*Voyage to Venus* (Pan, 1960)

That Hideous Strength: a modern fairy-tale for grown-ups (John Lane, 1945; abridged for Pan, 1955)

The Great Divorce: a dream (Geoffrey Bles, 1945; Collins Fontana, 1972)

Till we have Faces: a myth retold (Geoffrey Bles, 1956; Collins Fount, 1978)

The Dark Tower and Other Stories ed. Walter Hooper (Collins, 1977)

Boxen: the Imaginary World of the Young C. S. Lewis ed. Walter Hooper (Collins, 1985)

The Narnia Chronicles

The Lion, the Witch and the Wardrobe (Geoffrey Bles, 1950; Penguin/Puffin, 1959)

Prince Caspian (Geoffrey Bles, 1951; Penguin/Puffin, 1962)

The Voyage of the Dawn Treader (Geoffrey Bles, 1952; Penguin/Puffin, 1965)

The Silver Chair (Geoffrey Bles, 1953; Penguin/Puffin, 1965)

The Horse and his Boy (Geoffrey Bles, 1954; Penguin/Puffin, 1965)

The Magician's Nephew (Bodley Head, 1955; Penguin/Puffin, 1963)

The Last Battle (Bodley Head, 1956; Penguin/Puffin, 1964)

Poetry

Spirits in Bondage: a Cycle of Lyrics (Heinemann, 1919)

Dymer (Dent, 1926; republished, 1950)

Poems ed. Walter Hooper(Geoffrey Bles, 1964)

Narrative Poems ed. Hooper (Geoffrey Bles, 1969)

The Collective Poems of C.S.Lewis ed. Hooper (HarperCollins, 1994)

Letters

Letters of C. S. Lewis ed. W. H. Lewis (Geoffrey Bles, 1966; revised ed. Hooper, Collins, 1985)

Letters to an American Lady ed. Clyde Kilby (Eerdmans, 1967)

Mark vs. Tristram: Correspondence between C.S.Lewis and Owen Barfield ed. Walter Hooper (1967)

They Stand Together: Letters to Arthur Greeves ed. Walter Hooper (Collins, 1979)

Letters to Children eds. Lyle Dorsett and Marjorie Mead (Collins, 1985)

Letters: C. S. Lewis and Don Giovanni Calabria: a Study in Friendship ed. Martin Moyniham (Crossway, 1987; Collins, 1988)

C. S. Lewis: Collected Letters, ed. Walter Hooper

–Vol. I *Family Letters 1905–1931* (HarperCollins, 2000)

–Vol. II *Books, Broadcasts and the War 1931–1949* (HarperCollins 2004)

–Vol. III *Narnia, Cambridge and Joy 1950–1963* (HarperCollins 2005)

Diaries

All My Road Before Me: the Diary of C.S.Lewis 1922–27 ed. Walter Hooper (HarperCollins and Harcourt Brace, 1991)

Collections of Essays, Talks, Sermons

Rehabilitations and Other Essays (Oxford University Press, 1938)

Essays Presented to Charles Williams with others (Oxford University Press, 1947)

Transpositions and Other Addresses (Geoffrey Bles, 1949)= U.S.A. *The Weight of Glory and Other Addresses* (Macmillan, 1949; 1980)

The World's Last Night and Other Essays (Harcourt Brace, 1960)

They Asked for a Paper (Geoffrey Bles, 1962)

Screwtape Proposes a Toast (Collins Fontana, 1965)

Of Other Worlds: Essays and Stories ed. Walter Hooper (Geoffrey Bles, 1966)

Christian Reflections ed. Walter Hooper (Geoffrey Bles, 1967)

Undeceptions: Essays on theology and ethics ed. Walter Hooper (Geoffrey Bles, 1971), redistributed as:

–*God in the Dock* (Collins Fount, 1979)

–*First and Second Things* (Collins Fount, 1985)

–*The Grand Miracle* (U.S.A. Eerdmans, 1970; Ballantine, 1983)

Fern Seeds and Elephants and Other Essays on Christianity ed. Hooper (Collins Fontana, 1975)

Of This and Other Worlds ed. Walter Hooper (Collins Fount, 1982)

First and Second Things: Essays on Theology and Ethics ed. Hooper (Collins Fount, 1985)

Present Concerns ed. Hooper (Collins Fount, 1986)

Timeless at Heart ed. Hooper (Collins Fount, 1987)

Books About C. S. Lewis

Carpenter, Humphrey: *The Inklings* (Allen & Unwin, 1978)

Duriez, Colin: *The C. S. Lewis Encyclopedia* (Monarch, 1992, rev. Crossway, 2000)

Gresham, Douglas: *Lenten Lands: My Childhood with Joy Davidman and C.S.Lewis* (Collins, 1989)

Hooper, Walter: *C. S. Lewis: A Companion and Guide* (HarperCollins, 1996)

Manlove, C. N.: *C. S. Lewis: his Literary Achievement* (St Martin's Press, 1987)

Martin, Thomas L. ed.: *Reading the Classics with C. S. Lewis* (Paternoster & Baker Book House, 2000)

Sayer, George: *Jack: A Life of C. S. Lewis* (Crossway, 1994)

Sibley, Brian: *Shadowlands* (Hodder & Stoughton, 1985)

Websites

www.cslewis.org

http://cslewis.drzeus.net

www.narniaweb.com

www.cslewisinstitute.org

http://ic.net/ruerasmus/RAZ26.HTM